YOU
AND
YOUR
RETRIEVER

YOU
AND
YOUR
RETRIEVER

Ralf W. Coykendall, Jr.

DOUBLEDAY & COMPANY, INC., GARDEN CITY,
NEW YORK.

LIBRARY OF CONGRESS CATALOG CARD NUMBER 63–7707

To "Tiny" and his friends

Contents

Acknowledgments

I am deeply indebted to the many people without whose help this book would never have been written; each has a share in any success it may enjoy:

Richard Adams of The American Kennel Club, C. A. Griscom and the Labrador Retriever Club, Eloise Heller and the Chesapeake Retriever Club, Thomas Novak and the Golden Retriever Club.

Edith and George Murnane, Torch Flinn, Louise and Augie Belmont, Ann Fowler, Audrey Brokaw, George Gardner, Pert and Roger Vasselais, John Olin, the Judges, the Captains and their Guns.

Joyce McKee, Wally Johnson, and all who have paved the way so as to make a book such as this possible.

My patient family, without whose help there would be no pictures, no words, no book.

To each and all, thank you.

Preface

The advice and instruction that is included here must be tempered with humanity, not because it is a sound approach to training, but because it comes from the heart. Your retriever has much to learn from you, but if you are unable to understand his problems and enjoy his companionship, all your efforts will come to nought.

My retrievers are part of our family. They are honored guests and among our favorite friends. They have made a great contribution to our enjoyment of life. It is with these thoughts in mind that this book is written.

Ralf W. Coykendall, Jr.

I

Your Retriever: His Beginnings

This book is intended to assist you in training your retriever to be a *working retriever*. There is a good deal to be said for retrievers as bench and obedience competitors, and there is no doubt as to their complete satisfaction as pets. However, this volume is concerned only with their working ability. The task of retrieving pheasants in fields of corn, ducks in icy water, or both in field trial competition: this is the work of a retriever and the work he was bred to do. You will do well to keep this in mind as you set out to pick *your retriever*.

The following list, based on American Kennel Club registration figures, not only covers the various retriever breeds, but indicates their relative popularity as well.

Labrador Retrievers	67.1%
Golden Retrievers	25.4%
Chesapeake Bay Retrievers	5.5%
American Water Spaniels	
Irish Water Spaniels	
Flat Coated Retrievers	2.0%
Curly Coated Retrievers	

You will note that three breeds: Labrador, Golden, and Chesapeake retrievers: account for all but two percent of the registered retrievers. If you have not already decided which breed to choose you will do well to read the several *breed standards* and write the *breed clubs;* see the Appendix of this book.

No matter which of the retriever breeds you choose, you should give careful thought to the sex of your pup-to-be. There are many things to be said in favor of bitches as both pets and hunting companions, but for the person who wants a retriever to serve its intended purpose of retrieving, a male is the pup to choose: bitches have a habit of coming in season or having puppies at the most inopportune times.

The most important consideration in choosing any puppy is his or her background. This background is several things: the puppy's breeder, breeding, and registerability. Each of these is extremely important and lack of complete assurance regarding any of them is all the reason you need to look elsewhere for your retriever.

As you set out to purchase your retriever, remember that you are about to buy a potential friend and member of your family; and like all members of your family you want him to be healthy, happy and intelligent. These qualities are only going to be found in a well-bred pup from a reputable breeder who runs a sound and healthy kennel. It is most important that you deal only with a reliable breeder of retrievers. If you have difficulty in locating such a breeder, contact the breed club of your chosen breed (see Appendix) and they will be more than glad to assist you.

If you hope to get a puppy that will have an insatiable desire to retrieve, you had better look into his breeding, or family tree. A puppy's breeding is in his pedigree, and you as a potential buyer should ask for and expect to see the pedigree of any puppy you are at all interested in.

What will you find by looking at a pup's pedigree? First, you will find out if he and both his parents are registered with The American Kennel Club. If they are, each will have a registry number following his name. Any questionable fact about either parent's registry is all the reason you need to look for another pup.

A puppy's pedigree will also tell you what, if anything, his relatives accomplished during their respective careers. In this area of accomplishment don't be misled by titles that have no bearing on a dog's working ability. The titles that are of interest to you as a buyer are Field Champion and Amateur Field Champion: these indicate that in the background of your pup there is proven working stock. That, after all, is what you are interested in: a retriever that will retrieve.

What else should you look for in a puppy? Are there things

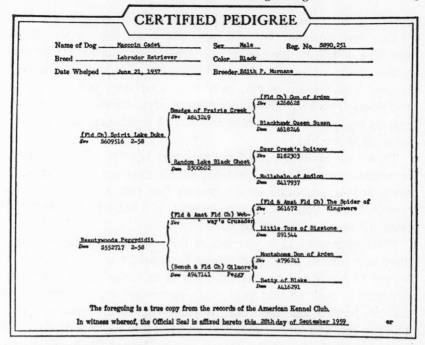

CERTIFIED PEDIGREE

Name of Dog ___Macopin Cadet___   Sex ___Male___   Reg. No. ___S890,251___

Breed ___Labrador Retriever___   Color ___Black___

Date Whelped ___June 21, 1957___   Breeder ___Edith P. Murnane___

Sire (Fld Ch) Spirit Lake Duke, S609516 2-58
- Smudge of Prairie Creek, A843249
  - (Fld Ch) Gun of Arden, Sire A268628
  - Blackhawk Queen Susan, Dam A618246
- Random Lake Black Ghost, S500602
  - Deer Creek's Doitnow, Sire S182303
  - Bullshalo of Audlon, Dam S417937

Dam Beautywoods Peggydidit, S552717 2-58
- (Fld & Amat Fld Ch) Webway's Crusader, Sire
  - (Fld & Amat Fld Ch) The Spider of Kingswere, Sire S61672
  - Little Tops of Bigstone, Dam S91544
- (Bench & Fld Ch) Gilmore's Peggy, Dam A947141
  - Montahome Don of Arden, Sire A796241
  - Betty of Blake, Dam A416291

The foregoing is a true copy from the records of the American Kennel Club.

In witness whereof, the Official Seal is affixed hereto this 28th day of September 1959   er

---

that will separate one pup of a litter from his brothers and sisters? In an older dog his desire to retrieve and general disposition will tell you much; however, the ideal age to get your retriever is when he is between six and ten weeks old, and at this age there is little to indicate which pup, or pups, will develop into the best retrievers. On the other hand, there are several things that you can and should look for. The puppy you pick should be healthy and alert, show an interest in his surroundings and have a degree of curiosity. As a general rule, pick the largest, yet most aggressive pup of the litter. Only time will tell if your choice was the correct one.

While there is no foolproof method of picking a retriever, a pup with proven background is very apt to be your best bet.

The list of retrievers on page 106, all of whom have proven their abilities by earning Field and/or Amateur Field Championships, should be of great value in your selection of a puppy.

Many questions will arise as you introduce your puppy to his new life. A new dog in the family is not unlike a new baby just home from the hospital. Your puppy, like a baby, needs a place that is all his own, and it should be ready and waiting for him.

The first question is: will your retriever live in the house with you or will he have a kennel? Unless there is something that makes doing so impossible, your retriever should have his own kennel. You, as the owner, owe it to your dog, your neighbors and yourself to keep him under control at all times. If he is to be kept in top physical condition and out of trouble, a kennel is the only place for him.

There are many types of kennels and equally as many styles of construction. They range from simple enclosures costing relatively little to elaborate establishments that cost a great deal. The type of kennel you build, or have built, is a matter of choice: the need for one is a matter of necessity.

Whether you build it yourself or have the work done for you, there are several important things to consider in constructing a kennel to house your retriever. First is to make certain that the structure is built so that your dog can neither dig nor jump out. Second, but no less important, is your dog's health and comfort. The run must be large enough to let your dog exercise freely, and be constructed of material that is easily cleaned. A long narrow run (four by sixteen feet or longer) with a surface of cement, gravel or sand is best. A house of some sort must be provided so as to protect your retriever from the elements. Third, but by no means least, you should consider yourself. You are the one who will have to feed your dog and clean his quarters. The kennel should be constructed so as to provide *you* with easy access.

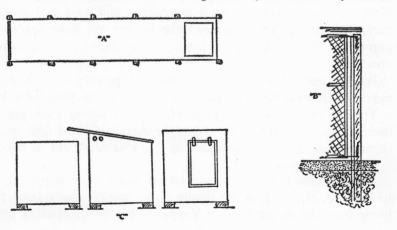

A minimum, yet sound and attractive kennel can be built as follows. The run should be approximately four by twenty feet. (See A, Diagram 1.) The important thing to remember is that the run must not allow its occupant to dig out, therefore the posts should be set two feet below the eventual level of the surface and the wire should then be fastened *to the inside* of the posts. (See B, Diagram 1.) The surface should be sand, crushed stone or concrete laid to a depth of six inches over stone or rock. The end of the run where the gate is to be should be reinforced to prevent digging out at that point. The gate itself should be made to fit and should have wire *on the inside.* It should then be secured to the posts with strong hinges and a lockable hasp. The top of the run should have a complete covering of wire securely fastened.

A house to protect your dog from the elements may be easily constructed of exterior plywood. (See C, Diagram 1.) Two important considerations here are proper ventilation and drainage. These are accomplished by providing small holes in the floor to let excess rain and snow escape and large holes in the peak to provide circulation of air. The entrance to the house should be over to one side so as to provide a dry, draft-free corner for your dog in cold or wet weather. A door may be added, but you will find that most dogs will delight in chewing on any flap or door you may provide.

The question that next arises is one of food and diet. What should you feed your pup? How often? Does he need vitamins or some other supplement in his food?

Some of these questions should have been answered by the person from whom you purchased your pup. Further information should be obtained from the one individual with whom you will entrust your retriever's health, your veterinarian.

There are several good, *name-brand,* dry dog foods that, used according to directions on the package, will maintain any puppy or dog in good health. The addition of meat or fat is advisable, but not necessary: today's dog foods are a complete diet, and in most cases further supplementation is wasted.

Your choice of a vet should be given just as much thought and consideration as would your choice of a family doctor. You are looking for a person with whom you feel your dog is safe, someone you are willing to trust without hesitation. Having chosen a veterinarian you should give careful thought to just when you will need his services. Aside from diet and the necessary shots and obvious emergencies that call for his assistance, consult your vet about your dog's loss of appetite, bad breath, poor coat and similar conditions. Other occasions that call for outside help will depend on your personal experience and knowledge. If a rule of thumb is to be established, it must be this: *any time you wonder about your retriever's health, don't hesitate—call your veterinarian.*

The next step in caring for your retriever is to see that his needs are properly attended to. These requirements are few, but they must be met. He must have fresh water always available, be fed at the same times every day and his run must be kept sanitary by daily cleaning. In addition to these daily tasks, there are others that need to be done every week or so. His bedding (cedar or straw) must be changed and his house cleaned out. The run and house should be sprayed every week in warm weather. (Ask your veterinarian about any spray before using it.) All in all, it is up to you to see that your retriever and his living quarters are maintained in a clean and healthy manner.

There now remains to consider your retriever's happiness. As a member of the family, he needs to be accepted on his own terms, not yours. He should have daily periods of exercise *out of his kennel.* These must be kept friendly and informal; there is time enough for serious training after your pup has gotten to know you and adapted to his new home and its surroundings. Be kind and patient; your puppy knows nothing and everything he does during these first days is done instinctively, not through any lack of training.

As you and your pup get to know each other, he should come in the house and be taken in the car occasionally. Both in the house and car, a young puppy can create a state of chaos unless he is under constant surveillance. In the house this presents no real problem; the car is another matter. While there is really no need for your pup to spend much time in a car at this early age, when he matures and you take him on trips, the car will become his home away from home. It is therefore important that he have a place in the car that is all his own.

Just as your retriever needs a kennel at home, he needs a "crate" in the car. It might seem unkind to house your dog in a box; actually just the opposite is true. Your pup will enjoy trips in his crate and you will have the security provided by knowing where your dog is and what he's up to; it tends to make for safer driving.

Again, just as was the case with various kennels, there are many crates available. They range from simple homemade plywood structures to the better, but more expensive, types con-

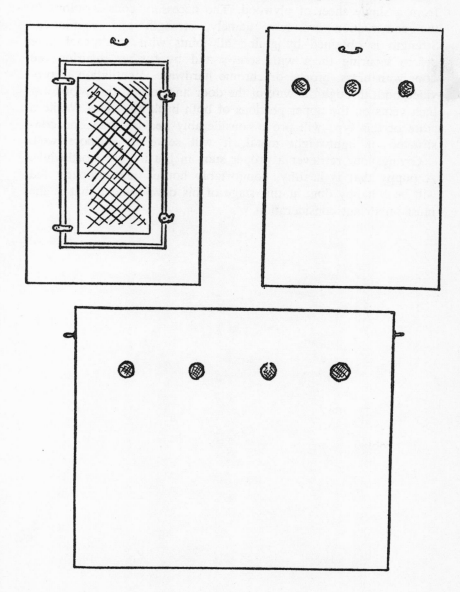

structed of various metals. The choice of a crate is up to you; the need for one is obvious.

A sound crate may be constructed of waterproof or marine plywood with relative ease and savings. Dimensions of twenty by thirty by twenty-eight inches high will afford your retriever all the room he needs to be comfortable, and the entire crate can be made from a single sheet of plywood. The necessary considerations in the construction are few, namely, strength and ventilation. Strength is obtained by gluing all joints with waterproof glue before securing them with screws and by further securing the door with brass, bronze or chrome hardware. Ventilation is provided both through the wire of the door and several three- or-four-inch vents on the upper portions of both back and sides. While a crate of this type will prove considerably heavier than one constructed of lightweight metal, it will serve its purpose well.

Giving your retriever a proper start in life is very worthwhile. A puppy that is healthy, comfortably housed and properly fed will be a happy dog; at this stage of his development that is the most important consideration.

II

Early Training—Obedience

Your retriever is properly housed and fed and you are ready to teach the little devil a thing or two. The question is, will he be ready to learn? Any dog over three months old is ready to learn, but training at this age, or any other age for that matter, must be kept in step with the dog's ability. Always remember that he is unable to reason and learns only by doing; it is therefore up to you to do all his thinking for him. Kindness and understanding are the keys to successful results. He wants to please, but you must show him how to do so. This chapter is devoted to equipping you with the necessary material and knowledge to train your dog; the proper approach is up to you.

The first step toward understanding and training your pup should be the careful consideration of his name. This is not only the first word that he will learn, but also the one that he will hear most often. Give your pup a name that is short and easily spoken, and one that will never conflict with other words that are apt to be used in his presence.

Consider for a moment the well-trained retriever who became completely confused whenever ducks approached his master's blind. Whenever ducks were sighted someone always called out "Mark," the signal that birds were coming. Unfortunately Mark was the dog's name. Obviously he was a very confused retriever. This illustrates the *great importance of a name*. Give it careful thought. Both you and your retriever will have to live with the one you choose.

In addition to his name, there are about a dozen commands

that your dog will have to learn. Some will prove easy to teach, others very difficult. *Each must be learned perfectly* if your dog is to become a working retriever, and they must be learned before he is taught to retrieve. These commands fall into two categories: necessary and secondary.

Necessary commands are those that your dog must learn in order to accomplish his appointed task of retrieving. They are: sit, stay, come, heel, kennel, leave it, hold it, drop it: and should be taught in that order.

Secondary commands are those that, although necessary, have no actual relationship to his working ability. These are: no, down, stop that noise, lie down, go on. You will find that some of these commands will all but teach themselves, while others will have to be taught early in the game. The order of teaching these secondary commands is a matter of personal convenience, but they must be learned perfectly.

Before taking your pup out for his first lesson you will need a certain amount of equipment. Each piece of equipment serves a definite purpose, and each will soon become as familiar to your dog as is his own name. For this reason you will want material that will last, and not inferior goods that will need frequent replacement. By purchasing the best, you will be saving money in the long run.

It is best to familiarize yourself with your equipment and its functions before putting it to use; for this purpose each item is pictured on Plate 9 and described here.

Choke collar. This is not at all what its name implies; it is not intended to choke your dog, but rather to be used as would any other collar, to fasten a leash to for the purpose of control. Its advantage is that, unlike other type collars that have a fixed size, it is flexible. When your dog pulls against the choke collar it tightens and becomes uncomfortable; he soon learns that he is only punishing himself. A choke collar should be of the proper size, just large enough to slip over your dog's head. One that is too large can injure your dog. Never let your pup wear a choke collar except when you are with him. If he is properly kenneled, which is where he should be when you are not with him, there is no need for a collar.

Leash. A short leash is used rather than a long one for an obvious reason: the closer your dog is, the easier he is to control.

A leash longer than eighteen inches will only prove unwieldy; in fact, an even shorter one is preferable. The leash you purchase should be of top-grade leather and have a brass snap firmly attached.

Belt cord. It is unlikely that anyone will know what you are talking about if you set out to purchase a belt cord by that name. The one pictured is actually a long leash with the snap removed; an equally good one can be made from a rawhide bootlace. The belt cord should be about five feet long and is used to restrain your dog when teaching him to retrieve. The procedure is simple and extremely effective; the loop of the cord is slipped under your belt, the other end is then slipped through the loop, thereby securing the cord to your belt. The free end is put through the ring on your dog's collar and held by you, making it impossible for your dog to leave your side until you drop it. Purchase or make a stout belt cord; you will find it a very useful piece of equipment.

Whistle. Make certain that you purchase several whistles; there are two good ones on the market, the Little Acme Thunderer and the Roy Gonia. It doesn't matter which you choose but be sure to purchase several; you will soon discover that whistles are far from indestructible and that they are an important part of your training routine. Purchase or make a cord on which to hang the whistle around your neck, where it belongs, always ready when you need it. Many people carry two whistles on the cord, one as a spare. While this is a matter of personal preference, the old adage that there is safety in numbers applies here.

Training dummy. These are in reality boat fenders and are used when teaching your dog to retrieve. These "dummies" are made in a variety of sizes and materials, but the ones you want should be three inches in diameter and made of canvas filled with cork, kapok, or rubber. It is a good idea to tie a short length of heavy cord through the eyelet of the dummy. This serves two purposes: it teaches your pup to carry the dummy with his head high, and it enables you to throw it more readily. When you begin field training you will need several training dummies, but for the time being one or two will serve your purposes.

As your dog progresses there will be other items of equipment that you will probably want or need, such as a blank pistol. But for the next few months, the equipment covered here—plus a patient attitude and a willing pupil—will suffice nicely.

Teaching your dog to sit is the first of all the many commands that he will have to learn. The ease with which he learns this first lesson should give you a clue to all his future training. If you encounter any serious difficulty at this stage of the game, you should analyze both your dog and yourself; one of you is not ready for the long road ahead. Perhaps your dog is not yet ready to be trained, or is actually untrainable. It is more likely, however, that you are at fault. Remember, patience, kindness and understanding are the keys to success.

If approached in the right way, teaching your dog to sit on command should take no more than a few short lessons. Start by making certain that you are where there will be no distractions. Put the choke collar on your pup and fasten the leash to it. Play with him for a minute or two while he gets used to this new sensation. Now, place your hand on his hips and press down firmly, saying "Sit" as you do so. If this does not force him into a sitting position immediately, exert additional pressure by pulling up on the leash as you press down with the other hand. This will force even a full-grown dog to sit. Don't have him sit for more than a second or two; release him immediately and praise him profusely. Repeat this routine several times, then quit for the day. Never let your dog become tired; the time to stop is while he is still ready for more.

You may or may not have to repeat this entire procedure during your next training session. Chances are that your pup has learned the lesson and will sit on command without any further pushing or pulling. If he does, all to the good; if not, you will have to keep at it until he does. Always praise your dog when he complies with a command; this is very important. Not only does your pup have to be shown what you want him to do, but he also has to know that by doing it he has pleased you.

When your pup sits when you tell him to without hesitation he is ready for the next lesson, but not before. He must learn each command perfectly before you undertake to teach him the next. This is important not only because each succeeding lesson is related to your dog's ability to comply with earlier commands, but also because you run the risk of confusing him if you try to teach him too much too soon.

The command "Stay" is actually a continuation of the lesson your dog has just learned. He will now be required not only to sit, but to remain in that position until released. The teaching procedure is simple, but putting it into practice will take time.

To teach your dog the command "Stay," start just as you did when you taught him to sit: collar on, leash attached and no distractions. Tell your pup to "sit"; with the leash held loosely, step close in front of him and tell him to "stay"; now, with the leash still held loosely, back one short step away from your dog, repeating "Stay" as you do so. Should he fail to remain sitting during this procedure, which is quite likely, go back to his side and repeat the entire routine. It will not be long before he understands that the command "Stay" means just that. As your dog progresses, drop the leash when you step away and increase both the distance that you back away and the length of time that you require him to remain sitting. Your ultimate aim is to have your dog "stay" when you so command, even though there are tempting distractions. Obviously this is something that cannot be accomplished in a few short lessons; it will take time. Here again, remember that impatience accomplishes nothing, while praise and understanding work wonders. When your dog will "sit" and "stay" for several minutes he is ready for the next lesson, but not any sooner.

The command "Come," if properly taught, should present no problems. In fact, it is the only command that your dog will really want to obey. "Come" is a command that your dog must obey whether it be spoken or whistled; he must learn that *two or more whistle blasts mean "Come"* just as the spoken word means the same thing. Be certain that in teaching this command you always use at least two blasts on the whistle; one blast will mean an entirely different command later in his training routine.

To teach your dog to "come" on command, start with the same familiar pattern that you used when teaching the last lesson. Have him sit, tell him to stay, and walk away from him. When you are about fifty yards from your pup, stop; blow two or more blasts on your whistle, call your dog by name and shout "Come." He'll do just that, it's what he wants to do anyway. Repeat this two or three times, making sure that he sits and stays until you whistle and command him to "come," and the lesson is all but learned. All that remains is to teach him to "come," not only when he wants to, but every time he hears the command. This is easily accomplished if, for the next few weeks, you never command your dog to "come" except when you are certain that he is ready and willing to do so. He will soon associate the command with something that he wants to do, and you will have circumvented the problems that arise when a dog is commanded to come while he is busy with other things.

Although most dogs learn to "come" without any difficulty, some will require a more emphatic approach. If this becomes necessary, the following method will quickly solve the problem.

Take your pup with his collar on to a large open field or lawn; attach a fifty-foot length of cord to his collar; hold one end and let your dog run. When he is some distance away, blow two or more whistle blasts, call him by name and command him to come. If he responds, all to the good; if not, jerk—don't haul—on the cord. A series of quick jerks will prove more effective than will a long tug-of-war. A few sessions with this, and the command "Come" will be implanted in his mind.

Before you teach your dog his next lesson, give some thought to the proper use of his name. In teaching him the last lesson you used his name in conjunction with the whistle and the spoken command, but it was used as a form of encouragement, not as a command. This is how you should always use your pup's name; use it when praising him, use it to release him from a given command, but never use it harshly. When you find it necessary to shout at your dog—and you will if you haven't already—substitute the word "you" for his name. In this way he will come to associate his name with pleasant happenings, and will therefore respond to it more readily.

A dog properly at "heel" is just that: he is neither ahead nor behind you, but even with your heels. For no reason is he to be allowed to deviate from this position; a dog that surges ahead or lags behind is not at "heel." Chances are that it will take time for your dog to learn to "heel" properly. Some dogs catch on to this command in a few lessons, but most require weeks of training; it all depends on the individual dog. In either case, this is a command that must be learned perfectly, and perfection can only be achieved through patience.

You must now decide on which side, right or left, you want your dog to "heel." The simple answer will depend on whether you are right- or left-handed. If you are right-handed your dog should "heel" on your right, the reverse being the case if you are left-handed. (As his training progresses and you teach him blind retrieves, you will find it far easier to give him an accurate line with the hand you use the most.) Once you decide where you will have your dog at "heel," that will also become the side on which he will sit when so commanded.

In teaching your dog the command "Heel" you will once again follow the now familiar pattern. With collar on and leash attached, have your dog sit on your right or left as previously decided. With the leash held loosely, walk forward and urge your dog to "heel." If he hesitates, as he probably will, snap the leash and repeat the command, adding both his name and the now familiar "Come." He will quickly understand that you want him to come with you, but he has no way of knowing that you want him to do so in a certain manner; this must be taught. Your dog will soon discover that the choke collar and leash prevent him from doing anything but accompanying you in the "heel" position; when he pulls ahead or lags behind, snap the leash and command him to "heel." He will eventually come to associate the command with the proper position by your side, but this will take time. This is a lesson your dog will learn only through repeated practice. When your dog "heels" perfectly on leash, try him with it off. If he shows no tendency to lag or wander, the lesson is complete. But remember, perfection is your aim and nothing less will suffice.

When teaching your dog a new command, never let him forget his previous lessons. Remember to practice the commands he has mastered, as well as the one you are teaching him during each training session. Your dog is a creature of habit, and habits are easily learned and just as easily forgotten.

Keep in mind that all work and no play tend to make for a dull dog. During your training sessions he is working for you; turnabout is fair play and it is up to you to show your pup that you appreciate him, not only for the work he does, but also because you like his company. He needs to be a member of the family. Take your pup for walks, let him go with you in the car, have him in the house in the evening; he needs this attention just as much, if not more, than he does his regular training.

By now you have discovered that some commands are easily taught and that others are difficult and time-consuming.

The command "Kennel," if properly approached, should be no problem at all. It means just about what it says: "Go into your kennel or any other place that you are so commanded." The method of teaching this command is simple repetition; each time you put him in his run or in the car, follow the same pattern. Have your dog sit; open the run or the crate door and tell him to "kennel." Chances are that he will obey willingly most of the time, but if he hesitates he must be forced to comply with the command. At the first sign of hesitation, force him bodily into his run or the car, as the case may be. He will very quickly learn that "Kennel" is one more command that must be obeyed.

The next lesson deals, for the first time, with a negative command, "Leave it." This covers a multitude of sins, such as telling him not to chase that cat or not to eat that cookie. In effect it is a mild form of the command "No." There is no special formula for teaching your dog to "leave it" other than its use and enforcement when applicable. This, like so many commands, is more easily taught when your dog is under close control; it is therefore advisable to have your dog on leash when you introduce him to the command "Leave it." Once you command your dog to do something, whether it be this or some other command, he must obey! If he finds out that he can get away with disobedience you are in trouble; therefore, think twice before you give your dog a command that you are not in a position to enforce. Remember, he is a creature of habit and it is up to you to make certain that all his habits are good ones.

Your dog should now be a good citizen and far better trained than the average pet. He should sit, stay, come and heel perfectly, and know what "Leave it" means. He also must know what "Kennel" means and that it, like the other commands, must be obeyed. He is by now a well-trained companion that you can take

*[handwritten note at top: * Do NOT use dummy for force training. Use stick taped at both ends.]*

anywhere without qualms. The next step is to teach him to become what his name implies, a retriever.

Before your pup can be expected to retrieve properly he must learn just what it is that he is to retrieve and how to do so properly. He must therefore become familiar with the training dummy and learn to handle it correctly. The next two commands, "Hold it" and "Drop it" both have to do with the training dummy and can therefore be taught at more or less the same time.

It is very important that your pup be introduced to the training dummy in the right manner; this after all is what he must retrieve —in training—for the rest of his life. He not only will have to retrieve literally thousands of dummies, but will have to want to do so. Therefore, proper introduction is all-important. Before insisting that your dog handle the training dummy correctly be certain that he has picked it up a few times and has decided that doing so is fun. Toss the dummy a few feet and let your dog retrieve it, clap your hands and kid him into bringing it to you; in other words, make a game of the whole thing.

Now, after your dog has gotten to know what the training dummy is and likes it, you may teach him to "hold it" and "drop it" on command. This is quite easily accomplished if done in a firm but friendly way. Have your dog sit, tell him to "stay"; take the training dummy and place it in his mouth, which is easily accomplished by pressing the skin of his lower jaw against his teeth. With the dummy properly placed in your pup's mouth, command him to "hold it" and prevent him from dropping it by holding his jaw shut. After a few seconds, release your hold, say "Drop it" and take the dummy from him. Chances are that he will all but spit it out, but if he wants to keep it don't jerk the dummy away from him; instead, squeeze his jaw and make him release it. Remember, he must learn to hold the training dummy firmly until commanded to "drop it," when he is to give it gently to you. Practice these commands a few times, but don't overdo it; they can be perfected during later training sessions. You want your dog to handle the dummy correctly, but you do not want to bore him. It is more important that he enjoy his work.

Before you teach your dog any actual retrieving work, spend a few lessons teaching him the secondary, or unrelated, commands and brushing up on the work he has learned. A little time spent on this work now will save you a great many headaches and much time later on.

The command "No" should be used sparingly and only when necessary; in other words, it should be reserved for the times when no other command will do. It should be considered a severe command by both you and your dog; "No" should be used in those cases where you are prepared to back it up with punishment. It is a word that is short and easily understood by your pup; once he associates "No" with your obvious displeasure, this lesson is learned.

This is a good time to consider punishment; it is something that is necessary on occasion. Punishment is something that can take many forms, from a mild reproach to a hard spanking; the proper form for your pup depends entirely on you and his ability to take it. Some dogs are never hit, while others thrive on it; actually something between these extremes will probably work for the average dog. The one important thing always to remember is never to punish your dog except when he knows why he is being punished; remember, he does not reason, and it is therefore necessary to catch him in the act if the punishment is to be effective. If your approach is kind and understanding and your pup has learned his lessons well, there should be few, if any, occasions when punishment is necessary.

Once your pup learns the command "Down" properly, you should never need to use it again. This command is very easily taught, but only when your pup actually jumps on you can you teach it. When he jumps up, grab both his front paws and pinch them, commanding "Down" as you do so. This same method is used to teach your pup not to paw you. Grab the foot and pinch it, saying "Down" as you do. It won't take your dog long to learn that you would prefer that he show his affection in another way.

The command "Stop that noise" meets a variety of needs and is easily taught. When your pup barks or whines unnecessarily, place your hand around his jaws, shake his head and command him to "stop that noise." If he fails to catch on to this after a few times, resort to more severe punishment. This is a command that your dog must learn, if for no other reason than the fact that both you and your neighbors appreciate a good night's sleep.

The command "Lie down" need be taught only if you feel that it is worthwhile. If your dog has been taught to sit and stay until commanded otherwise, he will eventually lie down of his own accord and there is no need to teach him to do so. However, the command is useful if you have your dog in the house frequently, and is easily taught. Have your pup sit, take both front paws in your hands and pull them toward you and command your dog to "lie down" as you do so. He will catch on to this in a hurry and the lesson is learned.

The next command is actually a release and one that should prove both useful to you and popular with your pup. When you tell your dog to "go on" you are telling him to do what he wants and that he is not expected to be under control. However, this does not mean that you should ever let your dog get beyond the limits of your control, or that he should be allowed to do any of the various things he has been taught not to do. To teach your pup what "Go on" means, all you have to do is use it. When you take him for a walk, wave your hand and say "Go on" in a friendly manner; he'll very quickly understand.

You and your dog will spend a good deal of time learning these commands, but more important, you will get to know each other. You will learn to understand your pup and he will learn to obey you without hesitation. His obedience and your understanding will both be more than useful in the months that lie ahead.

Intermediate Training
Marked Retrieves

When working with your retriever there are several things you must remember. He is young, and because of this is more or less unpredictable. It is a most unusual retriever that shows consistency before he is eighteen months old. Praise him, punish him, but *never push him* beyond his capabilities. By now you have taught your dog a certain behavior pattern. By this I mean that you have *taught him all the simple obedience* covered during his early training. He still has much to learn. He must be steady to shot and able to retrieve from both land and water. It is with these lessons that this chapter deals.

There are three simple but extremely important rules to follow when training your retriever. *1. Never let your dog break* to retrieve. This can't happen if you use the belt cord until he is steady beyond a shadow of a doubt. *2. Never give him a retrieve that he cannot do.* This is easily accomplished if you always keep your training in step with your dog's ability and development. *3. Never let your dog lose interest* in his work. Praise him when he works well, repeat the lesson when necessary, but above all, keep your training sessions short. It is far better to undertrain than to bore your dog.

During his early training you kidded your dog into picking up and returning the training dummy. Now he is ready for his first actual retrieve. There are predictable things you can expect him to do and by anticipating them you will be better able to cope with his actions. He will break when the training dummy is thrown unless prevented from doing so. Once he has picked up the dummy he will play with it rather than return it, and even after you have kidded him into bringing you the dummy he will not want to let you have it. Rather than taking these as separate problems, let's go through his entire first retrieve.

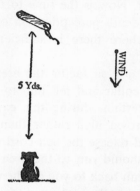

1. "His . . . first retrieve."

Take your training dummy, your belt cord, your whistle and your dog to a lawn or close-cropped field where there will be no distractions. Heel your dog and have him facing into the wind; slip the belt cord through his collar and say "Sit" firmly. Toss the training dummy upwind so it will land no more than five yards in front of your dog. If he tries to break while the dummy is in the air, restrain him with the belt cord and say "Sit" forcefully. As soon as the dummy is on the ground, release the belt cord, make an underhand gesture toward the dummy and *send your dog by saying his name.* He should run to the dummy and pick it up. As soon as he does, *blow your whistle twice* and run away from him as fast as you can. He will run after you; when he catches you, take the dummy from him by taking a firm hold on it and telling the dog to *"drop it."* Never jerk the dummy out of his mouth, always make him release his hold and give it to you.

There it is, just that simple. Your pup has completed his first retrieve, but it will take many sessions of repeating this routine before he will do it perfectly. Don't hurry him. Praise him when he works well, and stop before he shows signs of becoming either bored or tired.

During these sessions while you are teaching simple retrieves, don't let your dog forget any of his early training. Use it every day. When your dog "heels to" each training session, sits without any sign of breaking until you send him, picks up every dummy neatly and retrieves them neatly to hand, you are ready for the next step, not one minute sooner.

Up to now your training has consisted of only the simplest retrieves in open cover. Now is the time to teach your dog to use both his nose and his depth perception. In other words, it is time to move to a field where there is sufficient cover to hide the thrown training dummy.

 To start, have your dog sit facing the area of the fall, slip the belt cord through his collar and tell him to sit. Toss the training dummy upwind. Be certain, during this early training in cover, that the dummy is thrown high rather than far. As soon as the dummy hits the ground release the belt cord and send your dog by saying his name. He should run to the area of the fall, hunt for, and find, the dummy, run back to you on the whistle and deliver the dummy to hand. Practice these short retrieves until your pup is doing them perfectly. Then, and only then, increase the length of the falls and difficulty of the terrain. Remember, never push your dog beyond his current stage of knowledge and ability.

As the length of the falls increases you will need an assistant. Having someone other than you throw the training dummy is a new experience for your dog. For the first few retrieves expect him to run to your assistant rather than to the dummy. To correct this, have your assistant toss the first few dummies to land all but at his feet. In this way, when your dog runs to your assistant he will also be running to the training dummy. As he catches on, gradually increase the distance of the fall from both the dog and your assistant. Keep this up until he is doing perfect retrieves at distances up to one hundred and twenty-five yards. Do not, however, let him get in a rut. Never give him retrieves all the same length on any given day. If he is working well at eighty yards, train him at that distance, but give him some short work too.

When your dog is proficient on long retrieves it is time to introduce him to guns. Start with the blank pistol. Have your assistant, at a distance of fifty yards or so, fire the gun as he throws the training dummy. As your dog becomes accustomed to this new sound, gradually decrease the distance until the shot is being fired within a few yards of the dog. Introducing the gun in this manner, you should never have any problems with a gun-shy dog. He will associate the sound of guns with his work and it will sharpen his enthusiasm.

You will have to spend several weeks, probably much longer, training your dog to become steady to shot and to do single retrieves in cover to perfection. By perfection I do not intend to imply that any dog can do every retrieve perfectly, but he should be able to do a large percentage of them with style and speed. If not, perhaps you have expected too much and hurried your training. Slow down, decrease the length of the falls and stay with it. If after several more weeks of training he still shows no promise, it is probable that you are wasting your time on a dog that will never make a good shooting dog, let alone a field trial prospect. You should honestly evaluate the eventual success of your training program.

Doubles are the next step in your training. For these, go back to the lawn or close cropped field where you started his training on singles. It is a good assumption that although he is steady as a rock for singles, doubles will confuse him. Be prepared for him to break, and be ready to prevent it with the belt cord.

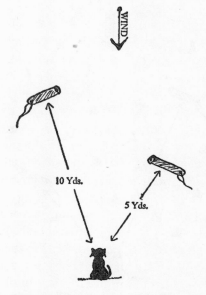

2. "Doubles are the next step. . . ."

Have your dog sit so that he is facing both into the wind and toward the area of the long fall, the first one thrown. This is the one he is apt to have trouble with. Slip the belt cord through his collar, *make certain he is facing the area of the long fall* and tell him to sit. Toss the first dummy about ten yards to the left, the second one about five yards to the right. Send your dog for the right-hand dummy with the underhand gesture and the use of his name. He will want to pick up this one first—it is freshest in his mind and closest. When he has picked up and delivered it, have him sit facing the left-hand dummy. Again use the underhand motion and the use of his name and send him for the left-hand fall; exaggerate the motion of your arm this time. He should have no trouble with this, but if he does, go out with him, show him the dummy and let him pick it up. Run back to the spot from which you sent him and take the dummy from him.

Your dog may catch on to doubles in a hurry or it may take weeks. In either case, stay with simple doubles that your dog can see until he is perfect. As he progresses, increase the distance of each fall gradually, always keeping the second dummy thrown closer to the dog than the first one. Remember, impatience on your part will only slow your dog's development.

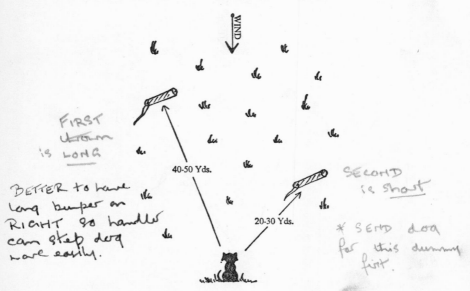

FIRST ~~DUMMY~~ is LONG

40-50 Yds.

BETTER to have long bumper on RIGHT so handler can step dog more easily.

20-30 Yds.

SECOND is short

* SEND dog for this dummy first.

3. "*. . . give him some that he can't see.*"

When your pup is doing visible doubles to perfection, return to the field with cover and give him some that he can't see. As he improves you will need two assistants, one for each fall. Have each assistant shoot and throw their dummy; <u>again make certain that</u> <u>the long fall is first, the short one last.</u> When your pup is doing near-perfect doubles in cover at distances up to one hundred yards, he has all but completed his land training. Now all that is necessary is to mix up the training routine while putting into practice everything your dog has learned thus far. In other words, keep him on his toes and strive for perfection in all you have taught him.

You should encounter no difficulty in teaching simple water retrieves. In many ways they are easier than those on land. They are more visible and should pose no problem, *provided your dog is completely at home in the water.* Some dogs will break ice to swim, others need an incentive even to get their feet wet. Few, if any, actually dislike the water, but some do need a certain amount of coaxing. If you have a dog that is just crazy about the water, go ahead and give him his first water retrieve. If, on the other hand, your dog has little or no water experience, take the time to introduce him to it properly.

There is really only one way to teach a young dog to like the water if he shows any doubts about it: go in with him. Put on your boots or bathing suit and take your dog to a calm pond or stream where there is a firm, sloping bank. Wade in the water and call your dog; sooner or later he'll join you. Keep this up until he decides that this is fun and is entering the water without hesitation and swimming around joyfully.

Your dog is ready for his first water retrieve. Follow the pattern which by now should be a habit. Have him sit facing both wind and water, put the belt cord through his collar and tell him to sit. Toss the dummy to land no more than fifteen feet away in shallow water. As soon as the dummy is on the water, release the cord and send your dog with the underhand gesture and his name. He should pick up the dummy with no difficulty; the only potential problem here is that he will drop the dummy to shake as he reaches shore. This can be prevented by meeting him at the water's edge and taking the dummy quickly. Each time he retrieves, step away from him, a little farther each time, until he is running to you to give up the dummy without any thought of shaking until the job is done. *Never let him drop the dummy to shake;* this can become an all but incurable problem later.

As soon as your dog is doing these simple water retrieves well, change your training area. Take him to a pond or stream with a steep bank. This will force him to leap into swimming water without any preliminary wading; he will encounter many situations where this is necessary and in a field trial dog it is all-important. Practice this type of retrieve until your dog is sailing through the air and hitting the water with a splash.

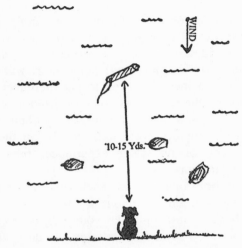

4. *". . . introduce him to duck decoys."*

By now, your pup should be leaping into the water and doing perfect single retrieves and this is the time to introduce him to duck decoys. All you will need are two or three decoys. Anchor each one separately on as short a line as the water depth will permit; you don't want your dog tangled up in excess line. Now do a simple water single. Toss the training dummy over and just beyond the decoys and send your dog. If he tries to retrieve a decoy say *"Leave it"* sternly. Repeat this as often as necessary until your dog shows no interest in the decoys. Once he has learned this lesson he should never again confuse a decoy with an object that he has been sent to retrieve.

With water entry and decoys behind you, follow the old familiar pattern. Lengthen the falls and introduce new and more complex training areas; here again, as the dog's ability increases and the falls get longer, you will need an assistant. When he is doing near-perfect work at distances up to one hundred yards, has no difficulty with the toughest marsh and delivers each and every dummy neatly to hand without shaking, you are ready for water doubles.

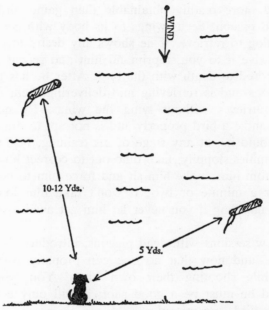

5. *". . . water doubles will be no problem."*

To introduce water doubles, go back to the pond or stream where water singles were begun. Follow the same procedure as with land doubles; the first one far, the second close. Always be sure that both are clearly visible to the dog. If your pup learned his earlier lessons well, water doubles will be no problem. Here again, as the dog's ability increases, use your assistants, lengthen the falls and introduce new and more complex training areas.

Your dog should now take both land and water in his stride and do perfect or near-perfect retrieves from both. He should heel and sit without signs of breaking until he is sent, and he is steady to shot. There remains only to maintain him at this high performance level and to introduce him to birds.

If you have difficulty locating birds for training purposes, contact either your local game warden or your State Fish and Game Department. They will be more than happy to assist you.

Do not let your pup pick up birds that have been shot for him until he has picked up a good many dead ones. For his introduction to feathers, use pigeons. They are small and easy for a young dog to handle and, perhaps more important, they are both cheaper and more readily obtainable than game birds. Take a freshly killed pigeon, tie its wings to its body with cord, and toss it for your dog to retrieve. If he shows any desire to play with it rather than give it to you, reprimand him and repeat the routine until he is bored to death with the bird. After he has gotten used to tied pigeons and is retrieving and delivering them nicely, give him some retrieves without tying the wings. By now he has learned to handle a bird properly and is not apt to drag one in by its wing. Should he, at any stage of his training, begin to handle birds or dummies sloppily, take time out to correct him. Take the bird away from him, make him sit and force him to hold the bird properly for a minute or two. It won't take him long to learn proper bird handling if you never let him get away with a sloppy job.

After a few sessions with dead pigeons, introduce live ones. Let me say here and now that no one can properly train a young retriever while shooting their own birds. You will need an assistant and he must be a good shot; it will only confuse your dog if many birds are missed.

Start live-bird training at forty or fifty yards and gradually increase the distance. For the first few retrieves be prepared for your dog to break and prevent it with the belt cord. Once your dog has become used to both live birds and the sound of a shotgun, have a bird thrown and shot right next to him. Make certain that your belt cord is both on and ready. Actually any dog that is proficient in marking training dummies will have no trouble marking birds.

Doubles with live birds are treated exactly as those with training dummies. It is not necessary to have both birds flighted and shot, although this is good to do occasionally. One dead and one live bird will suffice for most retrieves. Your dog will want to pick up the flighted and shot bird first, so plan your training accordingly; make this the close one.

The introduction of pheasants should be treated in just the

same manner as the first pigeon. Start with a dead one, tie its wings and proceed as with the first pigeon. After he is working well with the dead pheasant, give him a flyer. Have a bird flighted and shot right in front of your dog, but have your belt cord ready. Even though he has never done so before, your pup may try to break on this large and exciting bird. It is not necessary to spend much time or money training with pheasants, but they do serve a purpose. They teach not only a greater degree of steadiness but also the proper handling and delivery of large birds.

The introduction of ducks is the last, but by far the least, of the many things your dog has had to learn. After all, this is the bird he was bred to retrieve. Here again, start with a dead bird. Proceed just as you did with training dummies, taking care that your dog does not drop the duck at the water's edge to shake. After the first few retrieves, switch to shackled ducks—those with their legs and wings securely tied. It is also advisable to secure the duck's bill with tape or a rubber band; quite a few young retrievers are set back in their training by having a duck nip them. Shackled ducks serve several purposes. They teach your dog to handle cripples; they prepare him for possible field trial work, where they are used extensively, and they cut training expenses, as they can be used over again with proper care. At this last stage of intermediate training, again keep in mind: never give your dog any retrieves that you are not certain he can do.

At this stage your dog should heel perfectly, sit on command and be steady as a rock when a duck or pheasant is shot right under his nose. He must pick up land and water singles and doubles in the most difficult terrain and deliver them tenderly to hand. If you can honestly say that your dog does all these things, you have a retriever that you can be proud of—one that you can take hunting or enter in the Derby Stake at a field trial.

Advance Training
Blind Retrieves and Triples

Before you approach this stage of training, a word of caution: don't rush into new areas of training unless your dog has mastered all his previous lessons, and don't attempt to teach him new lessons until he has had time to fully digest the old ones. He needs time to put to use the many things he has learned. It is a good idea to give your dog a full season of hunting before you teach this advanced and complicated training. In this way he will become more competent in marking falls and less apt to forget this all-important training as he goes on to new fields of endeavor.

The teaching of "blind retrieves," those that your dog has not seen, is an arduous task, one that requires a patient attitude and a willing pupil. Your dog now has to learn that you are smarter than he, and he must be made to learn this in a way that will prevent him from losing interest in his work. The teaching of blind retrieves is far from simple, but there is a pattern that, if followed, will make the training easier.

There are three basic steps in teaching blind retrieves. All are very necessary and they must be taught in order. *Your dog must learn to stop, sit and look at you when you blow one blast on the whistle;* having done this [2] he *must then go in the direction you indicate with your hand,* and thereby locate the training dummy. After your dog has mastered hand signals [3] he *must then learn to go directly from your side toward a fall he has not seen*—this is called "to take a line." When mastered, this training will enable your pup, with the help of the line you give him and hand signals when necessary, to locate any and all falls, whether he has seen them or not. Rather than go into each of these steps as they relate to the end result, let's take them in their order of teaching; this, after all, is the manner in which your dog must learn them.

If your dog is ready for this advanced training, we must assume that he will both "sit" and "stay" when so commanded. This being the case, he must now learn to do just that, not only when the command is spoken but also when he hears one whistle blast. This is something that your pup will grasp more readily if the lesson is a continuation of an earlier command, rather than a new and baffling experience.

This lesson is much the same as were his earliest lessons. With your dog at heel, walk several steps, stop, and tell your dog to "sit"; blow one blast on your whistle, tell him to "stay"; and walk several paces away from him. Call him to you, praise him and repeat the whole procedure again, always being certain to blow one whistle blast between the commands "Sit" and "Stay."

In a few lessons your dog will have come to associate one whistle blast with both the commands "Sit" and "Stay" and should do just that when you blow the whistle, even though you do not speak. As soon as he sits and awaits further orders when he hears this whistled command he is ready for the next step, which, by the way, is the most important one in the entire routine.

Now is the time to test your dog. Will he sit and stay every time you blow your whistle? Will he obey the command at distances up to one hundred yards? If he does, that is all there is to this lesson; if he doesn't, now is the time to correct him. The very first time he disobeys the whistled command to sit, chastise him and make him comply; this will save a great deal of trouble as the days go on. Although it may seem unimportant now, your dog's compliance with the whistled commands to sit is the most important phase of teaching blind retrieves.

Your dog must now sit the *instant* he hears one whistle blast, and remain in this position until given further orders. When he does you may proceed to the next step, which is one that is apt to confuse you a good deal more than it does your dog, and for that reason is a phase of training that you need to practice before you try it on him. The best way to become a good handler is to know exactly what your dog sees when you give him a signal, and the best way to do this is to practice in front of a mirror before you attempt to teach your dog what you expect of him as you wave your hands madly in the air. One evening spent on this will be well worth the effort.

There are many hand signals that your dog will come to know, but for now content yourself with these: BACK, LEFT, and RIGHT. (See photographs following page 84.) Your dog should come when you whistle him in, so in reality he will be learning four signaled commands.

The next step is that of relating these hand signals to corresponding action on the part of your retriever. To do this properly you must have a pattern that you follow and one that your dog will soon learn to follow as readily. For this purpose we will use an imaginary clock.

1. BACK

Start with the command BACK. As in your earliest training sessions, take your dog, training dummies and whistle and go to a field where he can readily see the training dummies on the ground. Now set up your imaginary clock; have your dog heel to the center of the clock, <u>blow one blast on your whistle</u> and tell him to sit and stay. Toss your training dummy to land no more than ten yards away at what we will call twelve o'clock. You walk to six o'clock, making certain that your dog remains seated. Turn and face your dog. <u>Blow one more blast on your whistle to</u> get his attention, give him the overhand signal and tell him to "get back." He may hesitate, but it is not likely; he knows where that dummy is and will turn and run to it. Practice this a few times and your dog has learned his first hand signal, BACK. <u>Don't for any</u> reason give <u>him more than one signal to contend with on any of</u> <u>the first few days of this training.</u> Remember, this is all new to your dog. Now more than ever, patience and understanding are the keys to success.

? may be better to persist with back until dog can do a 100 yds + back before progressing to overs.

2. GET OVER *RIGHT*

When your pup has thoroughly mastered the command BACK, he is ready to proceed to the next signal, which is a right-hand over. This should be approached as was the last lesson—same imaginary clock with the dog at the center. This time toss the dummy to land at three o'clock. Walk back to six o'clock. Face your dog and blow one whistle blast and give the right-hand signal as you command your dog to "get over."

Again, practice until your dog does it perfectly <u>and</u> don't

confuse your dog by doing more than one hand signal on any
given day. If you feel you want to spend more time training, give
your pup some simple marked retrieves.

Your dog should now know two hand signals and be ready for
the third, namely, the left-hand over. The familiar procedure is
followed again; this time the dummy is tossed to land at nine
o'clock and the left-hand signal is given as you say "Get over."
As soon as your dog has perfected this he is ready to learn the
fourth and last signal.

If your dog has mastered the last three hand signals, there
should be no difficulty in teaching him to come in when so
signaled. He knows the whistled signal to "come" and now need
learn that this has two meanings: to come to you, and also to
come *toward* you.

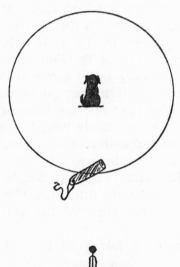

3. The signal to come in.

Again, the imaginary clock is put to use. With your dog sitting
at the center, toss the dummy to land at six o'clock. Now walk
on a straight line to and about ten yards beyond the dummy. Stop
and face your dog. Blow one blast on your whistle to get the dog's
attention, give him the hand signal to come in as you blow
several short, rapid blasts on your whistle. When he has mastered

this last signal he will know and respond to four hand signals: GET BACK, GET OVER (both left and right), and COME IN. You must now teach your dog that he is to follow orders and respond to hand signals whether he has seen a dummy or not; this will require both time and patience.

Hand signals and blind retrieves as your dog now knows them are really nothing more than a new way of doing marked retrieves. Although he responds to the signals you give him, he is actually only picking up dummies that he has seen thrown. It now is necessary that he be taught to do blind retrieves even though he has seen nothing. There is only one way to accomplish this— *Repetition*. Follow the same slow but sure routine as when you taught him his first marked retrieves. Keep distance and cover short and your patience long. Practice easy visible blinds that you have tossed until your dog is taking each and every hand signal perfectly. Then and only then is the time to test your dog.

Leaving your dog where he will not be able to see you, go out and toss a dummy to one of the four positions your dog has learned. Now heel your dog to the center of the imaginary circle, have him sit while you walk to your position at six o'clock; blow one whistle blast, give your dog the necessary hand signal and verbal command to the previously placed training dummy. If he has mastered the early stages of training, he will relate the signal to the corresponding direction he is to take and will thereby have no trouble locating the dummy. If your dog becomes confused, it proves that he needs more visual training. If he shows little or no hesitation, he has all but mastered the technique of blind retrieves.

Once your retriever is taking all four hand signals without having seen the dummy, there remains only to do as you did with marked retrieves: increase both the length of the blinds and the severity of the terrain. If your dog has difficulty in finding a blind you can now stop him with a blast of the whistle and direct him to the dummy with the necessary hand signals. One thing always to remember: your dog *must* stop and look to you for direction when he hears one whistle blast. Never let him disobey this command.

Your retriever should now stop when he hears one whistle and then take the hand signal given him. He now must learn to locate

Golden Retriever—Field Champion, Amateur Field Champion,
Canadian Dual Champion:
Rockhaven Raynard of Fo-Go-Ta,
owned by Mrs. George H. Flinn, Jr.

Labrador Retriever—1957–59 National
Champion: Spirit Lake Duke,
owned by Mr. and Mrs. George Murnane

Chesapeake Bay Retriever—Field Champion, Amateur Field Champion, Canadian Field Champion: Nelgards Baron "C.D.", owned by Mrs. Walter S. Helle

". . . a potential friend and member of the family."

". . . and have a degree of curiosity."

". . . should be healthy and alert, . . ."

There are many types of kennels in a variety of styles and sizes.
This is one of the more elaborate kennels, but the simpler ones
work just as well.

Every retriever needs his own kennel.
Here is a simple enclosure that is relatively simple to build and is inexpensive.

The car crate, ". . . his home away from home."

a blind starting from your side rather than from the center of the imaginary clock. He must learn to take a line.

Although you have always given your dog a slight line to his marked falls, he will in all probability be somewhat confused when you try to send him for something he has never seen. Don't let this happen. Teach your dog to take a line to a fall that he has not seen in a positive manner, one that utilizes not only his natural abilities, but all past lessons that will help as well.

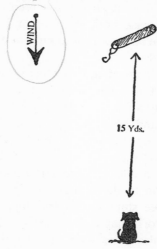

15 Yds.

4. ". . . a line to a fall . . ."

Just as with the more advanced blind retrieves, leave your dog where he cannot see you and toss a dummy to land where it will be easily visible and upwind of the position from which you will send your dog. Now, heel your dog to the predecided position so that he is facing into the wind and directly toward the dummy, which should be no more than fifteen yards distant. Don't hurry the sending of your dog, take plenty of time. Have your dog sit. With your arm, point directly at the dummy so that your hand is just ahead of the dog's nose. If he attempts to move his position, tell him to *sit* and *stay*.

There are two important things to check before you send your dog: is your hand pointing directly at the dummy, and is your dog's spine lined in the direction you are pointing? A dog moves in the direction his body is facing, not in the direction he is looking. If either your hand or the dog's spine is not correct, start

over. Have your dog heel, make him sit with his body facing the
fall and give him a careful line to the dummy with your arm and
hand.

Now . . . lower your hand slightly and send your dog by using
both his name and the command "Get back" as you raise your
hand. He should run out and retrieve the dummy; after all, he will
not only be able to see it, but scent it as well. Although this may
all seem like a great deal of effort, it is well worth it. Your dog
has taken a line to a fall that he has not seen. Here, just as with
all earlier training, increase both distance and type of terrain as
your pup progresses. He will soon be taking and holding a line for
longer and longer blinds.

Up to this time each step of training has been taken separately;
it is time to couple the three stages of training that he has
learned. Hide a dummy sixty or seventy yards away in moderate
cover. Heel your dog and have him sit facing the blind and give
him a line to the dummy, but . . . when he is about halfway to
the blind blow one blast on your whistle and *make* him stop, sit
and look at you. Give him the signal and command to get back,
and let him continue on to the dummy. He now has had his first
lesson utilizing all three steps of his training. There is little left
now but to give him work that will enable you to put all the steps
together. Give him false lines to falls and then stop him and
handle him in to them; set up your training so that you will be
able to use all that he has learned.

Teaching your dog to handle and do blind retrieves in the
water should present no problems. He has all the necessary
knowledge and training; only the element is different. If you start
with warm water and simple work, your dog should have no
trouble in relating what he has learned to do on land to its
equivalent in the water. Follow the same routine you used when
teaching him land blinds, increasing the severity of terrain as you
progress. Here, as in all other phases of training, patience and
understanding will work wonders.

Your dog, having learned to stop on the whistle, obey hand
signals and take a line, will probably have forgotten how to mark.
This is to be expected, and it is up to you to help him regain his
confidence; this is why the teaching of triples was left until last.

Teaching your dog to do triple retrieves will be relatively
simple, or very difficult; there is no middle ground. The answer is

entirely up to your dog; some dogs can count to three, others can't; the ease of training will be determined by this, and by this alone.

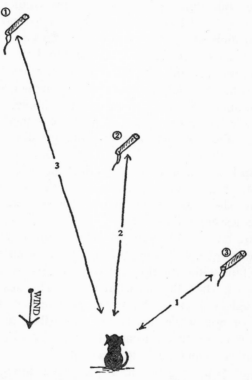

Triple retrieves should be started in the same place, and in the same simple way, as when you taught your pup his very first single and double retrieves. In other words, this work should be started in an open field or lawn where all three falls will be clearly visible to your dog. Have your dog sit facing both the wind and the area where the dummies will land. Toss the first dummy to land about twenty yards from your dog and to his left, the second about fifteen yards in front and the third about ten yards to his right. As you toss the dummies make certain that your dog is steady and that he has had time to see each one clearly. When the third dummy is down, send your dog *for that fall* with the underhand gesture and the use of his name. After he has retrieved it, have him sit facing the middle dummy, the second one, and send him *for that fall* in the accustomed manner.

He should have no difficulty with this. With the first two dummies retrieved, there remains to get the third one; your dog either will or won't remember that it is there. Have him sit facing the remaining dummy, take your time and see if he shows indications that he knows it's there. Send him for it. If he runs to and retrieves the dummy, your first attempt at triples is a success; on the other hand, if he becomes confused, help him find it. Walk out and show him the dummy and let him retrieve it. *Do not handle him;* if you do he will never learn to do triples. Whether your dog nails the three dummies or not, practice with simple, visible triples until your dog has proved to you that he either can or can't count to three; the next step of your training will be based on this decision.

If your pup has picked up all three dummies each time, you can go on to longer and tougher triples. On the other hand, if he has failed to show an ability to do triples you will have to approach his lessons differently.

If your dog has trouble with triples, you have several choices. The first, and most obvious, is to forget them; your dog is able to retrieve two falls without help, and you can always handle him to the third if and when the occasion arises. The next choice is to fight it through and make the so-and-so count to three whether he wants to or not; while this is not impossible, it is a long and very tedious method. In most cases it would be wise to accept the fact that your dog can't count to three and let it go at that. If you feel you want your dog to do triples even though he has no memory of the third bird, it can be painstakingly accomplished by teaching him to line to the fall. This is done in much the same way as was the teaching of blind retrieves. Only now he will pick up the two dummies he has marked and then, having forgotten the third, will learn to *take and hold a long line* to the remaining fall. The teaching is simple; putting it into practice may take a good deal of time and effort. It is a method that is a waste of time for all but those few retrievers that do just about everything else perfectly.

Your dog's formal education is all but complete; he has learned his lessons and now needs only to put his knowledge to use. Is he a fully trained retriever? Only you can answer that question.

Your retriever has learned the many obedience commands, does both marked and blind retrieves with enthusiasm and exactness, and delivers all birds tenderly to hand. He is steady under all trying circumstances and is a pleasure to you, his owner. If these qualifications accurately describe your dog, then for all intents and purposes he is a fully trained retriever.

Hunting with Your Retriever

Hunting with your retriever should be an experience that you enjoy together. It is your responsibility to see that such is the case. Your retriever is not a machine, but a flesh-and-blood animal that is ready and more than willing to work for you. You must be prepared to do the same for him.

When setting out on a hunting trip be sure that you have given careful thought to the needs and comfort of your retriever. He needs a warm, dry place to sleep. A "crate" and an ample supply of dry bedding will give him just that. Don't expect to buy dog food along the way; your pup is used to a certain diet and it is up to you to provide it. He will eat more when he is working hard all day than he normally does at home and this should be allowed for. If there is any question as to the availability of fresh water be sure that you have an adequate supply with you. It is also a good idea to carry a first aid kit for your dog with you. The items in it will vary depending on where you hunt, but a mild all-purpose antiseptic, an eyewash for seeds and pollen, and tweezers for thorns are things that are always useful. A snakebite kit may be added or not as conditions dictate.

Your next consideration is his mental well-being. This is an unending area of responsibility and one that is ever changing. Anything that is new to your dog must be considered by you before your dog encounters it. It is your responsibility to see that your retriever does not become frightened of something just because in your anxiety to get going you have neglected your dog.

While it is impossible to foresee all the unusual things a retriever is apt to encounter, some of the more common ones are
easily foreseen and solved before they become problems.

Boats are probably the most common single item that might
spook your retriever if he is not introduced to them correctly.
As soon as your pup finds out that boats are related to going
hunting, he'll beat you to the boat every chance he gets. However,
the time to introduce him to boats is not some morning in the
dark on your way to a day's shooting, but well before the season
opens in full daylight. Take time to take your pup for a boat ride;

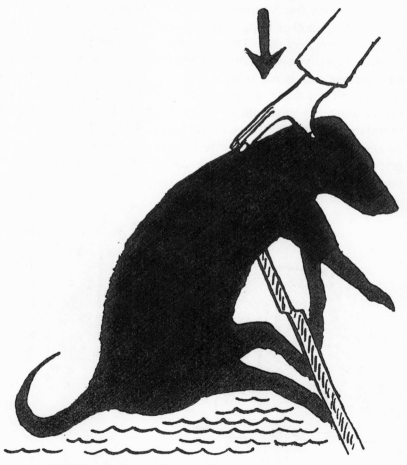

1. ". . . help him by pressing down on his head."

he'll enjoy it and you will have prevented a possible problem from ever occurring.

You will quickly find that your retriever will readily jump out of a boat to retrieve, but then have trouble getting back into the boat. This is something to work on. After your dog has returned to the boat with the bird or dummy as the case may be, take it from him while he is still in the water. Then, as he struggles to get into the boat and gets his front legs and head over the side, help him by pressing down on his head. This may seem odd, but you are actually giving him the necessary leverage that will enable him to get aboard. Don't try to lift him. It is all but impossible and you will quite likely find yourself in the water with your retriever.

Docks are another thing that will bother your retriever the first time he encounters one. Just as cattle guards keep animals from crossing them, you will find that your pup will be loath to walk on a surface that is not solid. This will soon be forgotten as your retriever relates docks to boats and boats to hunting, but for the first encounters you should expect your pup to balk when it comes to walking on a dock. There is no real problem here and therefore no need of a cure. When your retriever first encounters a dock, be prepared; have him on his leash and coax, don't force, him to come with you.

2. ". . . *a portion of the blind that is his exclusively.*"

Blinds, while they do not pose the problem that boats and docks do, should have your careful consideration insofar as they will affect your retriever. Your dog is in the blind for a purpose, to retrieve fallen game. It is up to you to see that he is in a position to do this without spooking incoming birds, disturbing you or running the risk of being shot. This may seem a big order, but it is easily accomplished if given the proper thought beforehand.

If you are building your own blind you should allow your retriever a portion of the blind that is his exclusively. In this way he will be able to see all that is going on and will be able to enter and leave the blind when ordered to retrieve. If you are not in a position to control the construction of the blind, you should size up the one you are to use before shooting from it, your objective being to ascertain where your retriever might best be located so he will be safe, comfortable and able to see any birds that are shot. You will find that a little thought and consideration will make a day in the duck blind more pleasurable for your retriever and more profitable for you.

3. *". . . rig your decoys separately and on as short lines as conditions permit." (A rather than B)*

Decoys are your next consideration. Your pup long ago learned that he was not to try to retrieve those wooden ducks. It is now up to you to see that he doesn't do just that. If you are a dyed-in-the-wool duck hunter you have probably always rigged your decoys with long lines or in multiples of some type. You will have to change your ways. If you expect your retriever to swim through your rig without disturbing it you will have to rig your decoys separately and on as short lines as conditions will permit. While this may add to the time it takes to set out and pick up your decoys, the time will be more than saved as your dog retrieves fallen ducks easily and without becoming wrapped up in unnecessary lengths of anchor line.

If you choose your hunting companions carefully and if your approach is kind and considerate, your retriever will have no serious trouble with anything he may encounter. Always remember, your retriever's only concern is to please you; it is up to you to be deserving of this adoration. He is dependent on you, not only for his room and board, but for his happiness as well.

You have probably heard it said that a retriever can learn to work game in the field as well as a spaniel. While this at least in part is true, you should consider this use of your retriever carefully before you attempt it. Basically a retriever is just that, a dog whose purpose it is to retrieve fallen game. Before attempting to alter this natural ability, consider the end result carefully. If you train your dog to find and flush game there is no doubt that it will impair his marking and retrieving ability. There are therefore two considerations you must not overlook. If you teach your dog to work game before he has thoroughly mastered his retriever training it is doubtful he ever will mark well. It is advisable to give him a hunting season of work before attempting any new lessons. If you hope to use your retriever in field trials, never teach him to work game. It will weaken his ability to mark and subsequently his chances to make the grade in a highly competitive sport, one where little things separate winner from also-ran.

With your mind made up, teaching your retriever to work cover as does a spaniel is reasonably easy. You will rely on his natural abilities and his complete mastery of his early lessons for this advanced form of training. If you have any doubts as to his steadiness or his handling ability, now is the time to give him a refresher course; both these areas of early training are of utmost importance if your retriever is to master this new lesson well.

The procedure to follow in teaching your retriever to work cover and thereby find and flush game is this: Take several pigeons, an

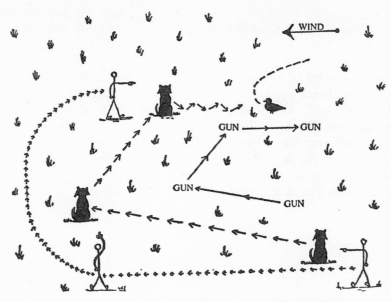

4. *". . . work cover as does a spaniel . . ."*

assistant to shoot the birds and your retriever to a field where there is sufficient cover to hide the pigeons. Place a "rocked" pigeon— one that has been spun until he is dizzy—out in the field in a spot you can easily identify and remember. This is done while your dog is kept where he cannot see what is happening. Next, get your retriever, and with you handling the dog and your shooting assistant keeping pace, work your dog in a long circle that will position him downwind of the planted pigeon. He will scent it, and expecting to retrieve, will go to the bird. This is the most critical moment. The pigeon will flush and your dog will want to give chase. It is up to you to see that your dog remains steady when the pigeon flushes; if he does, your assistant may shoot the bird and your pup be sent to retrieve. On the other hand, if your dog breaks, the bird must not be shot; put the dog back in the crate or car, plant another pigeon and try again. Your pup will soon learn that this is a game that is fun, but he will also learn that it must be played your way. Once your pup has learned to flush pigeons and remain steady during their flight, it is time to try the same procedure substituting pheasants or quail for the pigeons. The only difference here is in the degree of steadiness required of your retriever. As this lesson is mastered, you will find that you have a dog that can not only retrieve fallen game, but find it and flush it as well.

Again a word of caution: never let your dog break to retrieve. A dog that breaks, whether it be in the duck blind or field, is a hazard not only to himself, but to those with him and their enjoyment of the day's shooting.

Your retriever has taken another step along the unending road to perfection. He will always be ready and willing to learn new lessons; be certain you are there to see that each is properly initiated and that it is enjoyment rather than work.

VI

Retriever Field Trials and the Field Trial Retriever

Retriever field trials are one method of putting your months and years of training to enjoyable use. If you feel that this is a sport that might be of interest to you, it will be worth your time to familiarize yourself with all the many facets of this highly competitive sport. This chapter will give you some idea, not only what to expect at a field trial, but what a field trial will expect of you and your retriever.

Retriever field trials fall into three basic categories: *fun* or *picnic* trials, which are, as their name implies, informal; *sanctioned* trials, sanctioned by The American Kennel Club and by nature more serious in their intent; and *licensed* trials held under The American Kennel Club license, the trials at which retrievers are able to earn points toward their potential championships.

Whether a trial be formal or not, there are only three types of stakes that you are apt to encounter at any of them: those that require an experienced retriever, those for young dogs, and the informal stakes for inexperienced dogs and puppies. The following chart outlines the type of work your retriever will be expected to do in each of the various stakes.

If, with your help, your retriever has *mastered* the many stages of his training, there is no reason why you should not feel free to enter him in a retriever trial. *But* you owe it to both yourself and your retriever to go to at least one trial as an observer first. In this way you will be better equipped for competitive sport.

At your first field trial you will quite naturally be inclined to spend much of your time watching the competing dogs. This is

REQUIREMENTS

STAKE	STEADY	SINGLES	DOUBLES	TRIPLES	HONOR	BLINDS	
Puppy		X	X				note 1.
Gun Dog	*	X	X				note 1.
Novice	*	X	X				note 1.
Derby	X	X	X				note 2.
Qualifying	X	X	X	X	X	X	note 2.
Amateur	X	X	X	X	X	X	note 2.
Open	X	X	X	X	X	X	note 2.

*Steadiness is not normally a prerequisite in these stakes, but any well-trained retriever should be steady.

1. These are informal, non-regular stakes and the work that is required will vary in different areas.

2. These are regular, official stakes; a more detailed description will be found in the AKC Rules governing retriever trials reprinted in the Appendix.

fine and good, but there are other things that are of interest and important to you if you have any interest in these trials.

Basically a field trial is a group of people pursuing a sport they enjoy. If you look no further, the mechanics of such a trial are rather simple. Close examination, however, will reveal that it is the inner workings of a trial that make it tick, and these inner workings are another matter—one with which you should concern yourself if you intend to follow the sport beyond these pages.

Judges, guns, bird boys and the seemingly unimportant committee members—all are part of any trial, part of the inner workings. Without them there could be no trial. The importance of these people will be more easily understood if you consider the various tasks each must do.

Judges at a retriever trial not only are called upon to judge

BLACK DUCK   GADWALL ♂

♂   MALLARD   ♀

♂   PINTAIL   ♀

EUROPEAN WIDGEON ♂   ♀   BALDPATE   ♂

♀   SHOVELLER ♂   ♀   BLUE WINGED TEAL ♂

GREEN-WINGED TEAL ♂   CINNAMON TEAL ♂

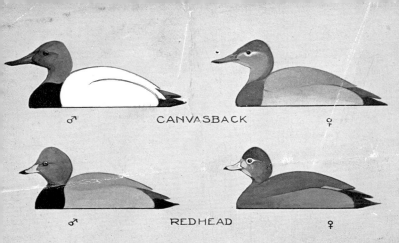

♂   CANVASBACK   ♀

♂   REDHEAD   ♀

♂   RING·NECKED DUCK   ♀

♂   LESSER SCAUP   ♀

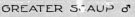

GREATER SCAUP ♂   BARROW'S GOLDEN·EYE ♂

♂   AMERICAN GOLDEN·EYE   ♀

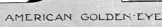

all the competing dogs, but are expected to set up fair, yet exacting tests on both land and water that will give each and every dog an equal chance. This is no easy task. Each test must be thought through with the end result in mind. No test should be such as to make it all but impossible for the dogs to complete. At the same time no test should be so simple as to make a comparison impossible. To this end the Judges are hard put to set up tests that will, in the course of the trial, give each dog a chance to prove his or her worth. *A more detailed concept of what any given Judge, or Judges, is seeking in their final placements may be gleaned from the* Standing Recommendations of the Retriever Advisory Committee, *which is in the Appendix of this book.*

All in all, you will do well to consider *why* the Judges have set up any given test just the way they have. Their reasons will become obvious only when you consider their motives. This is one of the many things you, as a relative newcomer to the sport, must observe.

While Judges would seem to be the most important factor at any trial, this is not entirely true. Without the services of competent Judges no trial could exist; by that same token, without competent assistance no Judge could judge, nor would there be any trial for him to judge.

Guns and the bird boys who assist them, while not actually involved in the competition, are a must at every trial. Only the finest shots in the area are asked to shoot at a retriever trial. The reasons for this should be obvious. If each dog is to be given an *equal* chance, the birds that are shot for him must also be equal. To this end the Judges will expect both the bird boys and the guns to give each and every dog equal throws and falls: only well-trained bird boys and the finest of shots are able to measure up to these rigid standards.

The tasks of Judges, guns and bird boys are easily seen if you take time to look. Not so the work of the field trial committee. They are the unsung workers who arrange all the details of the trial. *Their responsibilities are covered in the AKC Rules listed in the Appendix.*

Consider the many thankless responsibilities of the people behind the scenes at a retriever trial. You will soon see that it takes more than retrievers to make a retriever trial. Many interested and devoted people are necessary if such a trial is to exist at all. The part you play in this picture is up to you. It is quite possible that field trials will hold no interest for you. On the other hand you may be hooked, and a devotee of the sport for life.

Your next consideration should be the competing dogs and their handlers. How do you and your retriever stack up against the competition? This is a question only you can answer, but it is one that you must answer honestly. Only the best retrievers competently handled ever can hope to hold their own in field trial competition.

You must ask yourself, what is a good field trial retriever? What are the qualities that separate one dog from the others? The answers to these questions are in part covered in the *Standing Recommendations of the Retriever Advisory Committee* as listed in the Appendix. This will tell you the qualities, both good and bad, that judges are looking for in the competing dogs at any trial. You will quickly see that many things are required in the makeup of a successful field trial retriever. If there is one quality above all others that is necessary it is *consistency*. All other attributes become incidental if a dog never completes a trial. The dog that completes nearly every trial and is in there at the end *is a good field trial retriever*.

You better than anyone else are able to appraise your retriever. If you have trained him well and feel that he has what it takes to become a good field trial retriever, you may be right, but you'll never know until you enter him in a trial.

A word of caution: even the best retriever needs a good handler. It is up to you to be just that. You will be up against proven field trial competition, dogs and handlers that also believe in their chances. Try to remain calm; your dog will sense any nervousness on your part. Wait for the judges to call your number before you send your dog, and mark your falls carefully. A good handler will know when and how to help his dog when the occasion arises. Retriever trials are won by *good* retrievers *competently* handled.

If you are able to enjoy a trial, win, lose or draw, and even more important, enjoy your retriever in spite of his lapses, then perhaps you and your retriever will become a combination that is hard to beat. Only time will tell.

VII

Field Trial Tests

This chapter is intended to serve not only in helping you prepare your retriever for field trials, but also as a guide for anyone
who wishes to have his dog ready to cope with all situations,
whether they occur at a field trial or in a day's hunting.

If field trials are your aim, you should become familiar with
their workings and even attend an actual trial. On the other hand,
if your interests are strictly those of a hunter, you have probably
skipped over the areas of this book that deal with field trials
and are about to do the same with this chapter. Don't, not if you
want a well-trained retriever.

The tests in this chapter, while they are based on field trials,
depict situations that can and do develop under normal hunting
conditions. That, after all, is the theory under which field trials
are set up. You may not be able to duplicate each test as it is
shown, but you can approximate them. Each test will serve to
introduce both you and your retriever to some of the pitfalls and
complexities that dot the road ahead. It matters not whether said
road leads to a field trial or to a day in the duck blind.

DERBY TESTS

Long Land Single: Stubble and Brush

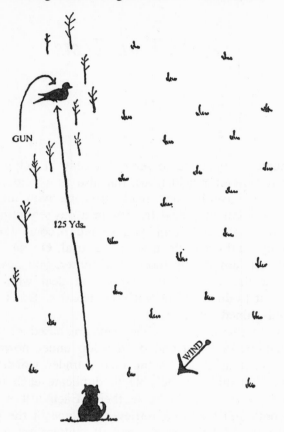

Except for the distance involved, this looks quite simple. Such is not the case. If the dog takes a good line to either the fall or the guns, he will wind the bird and have no difficulty, but in doing this he will have to leave the security of the field and enter the heavier going in the brush. The average dog will skirt the fall by avoiding the brush and will therefore be upwind of the bird and overrun it. This is a good but difficult test for a young dog—one that requires a good line and a degree of courage.

Land Double: Grass and Brush

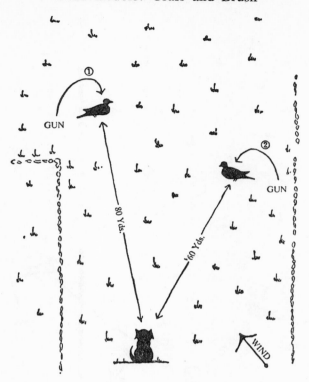

This test, like the first one, presents no problems for the dog that takes a good line to his falls, but unlike the first, the dog that avoids the cover will have less trouble than one that becomes interested in it. If a dog goes to the cover along the stone wall on either bird, he will be upwind of the fall and in trouble; such is also true of a dog that goes to the guns in either case. Although this is a fair test in every sense of the word, it is one that puts various temptations in the dog's path.

You and Your Retriever

Land Double: Low Stubble

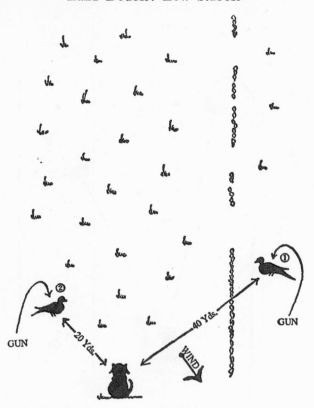

Another double, but one with a more subtle hazard. The short left bird is one that no dog should have trouble with. The right-hand bird presents a different problem. This too is a short bird and one that the average dog is sure he has marked. In fact, the average dog has marked this bird well, but the stone wall is there for a purpose and it serves this purpose well. It is an unusual Derby dog that doesn't look for an easy route through the wall. The route is there and when the dog finds it he has not only lost his line, but is upwind of the bird and in trouble.

Water Double: Swimming Water

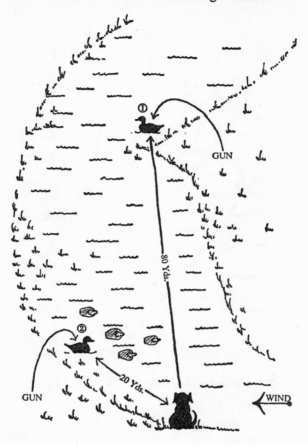

This test might well be described as a bank-running test. The short, left-hand bird is hard for a dog to miss even if he runs the bank. Not so the right-hand bird. A dog that runs the bank without a positive purpose is in trouble here, and it is a rare young dog that can resist that tempting bank as he swims toward that oh so distant bird.

Water Double: Wading, Swimming Bog

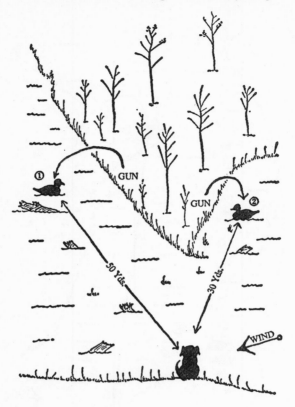

This test, like the last, is a troublemaker for the dog that prefers land to water. Few dogs will have any difficulty with the right-hand bird, but those who have a tendency to return to the point rather than swim the difficult route to the left-hand duck will be in trouble. They will be not only upwind of the fall but will tend to hunt the shore rather than look for the duck in the stump-infested water where in fact it is. In addition to the hazards presented by the tempting shoreline, some dogs will be confused by the many stumps and logs that dot the direct route to each fall.

Water Double: Swimming, Wading—Tall Reeds

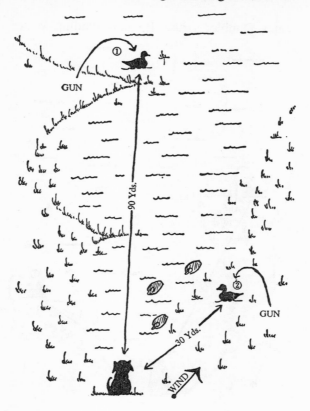

Another water double, but one of many complexities. A dog taking a good line to the short, right-hand bird will find it with little or no difficulty, anything less than a good line will find the dog in serious trouble. The short fall retrieved, there remains the long bird, and this presents a multitude of problems. A dog taking a direct line to the fall will cross the first point and in most cases hunt far short of the fall, while a dog that runs the shore will be upwind of the bird and will overrun it. This is a double that tests a retriever's depth perception to the fullest.

QUALIFYING TESTS

Water Double: Brush Points—Wading Water

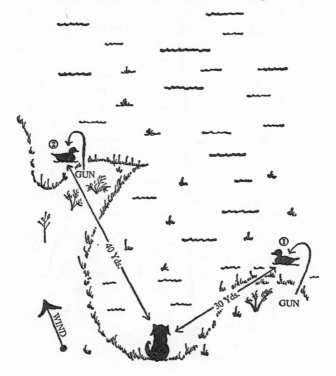

Yes, still another water double, but one beyond the capabilities of Derby dogs. This is a bank-running test where every dog will do just that—he'd be a fool if he didn't. A direct line to both right- and left-hand birds will take the dog across some land. The tendency is therefore to take the land route all the way to the area of the fall. While this in itself presents no problems, the fact that the dog has avoided water at the start does. The average dog has a tendency to continue along his original course, having once decided on it; in this case that means that he will run the bank beyond the falls, be upwind of the ducks and be in trouble. This is an easy test to set up, and one that it would be well to train on from time to time.

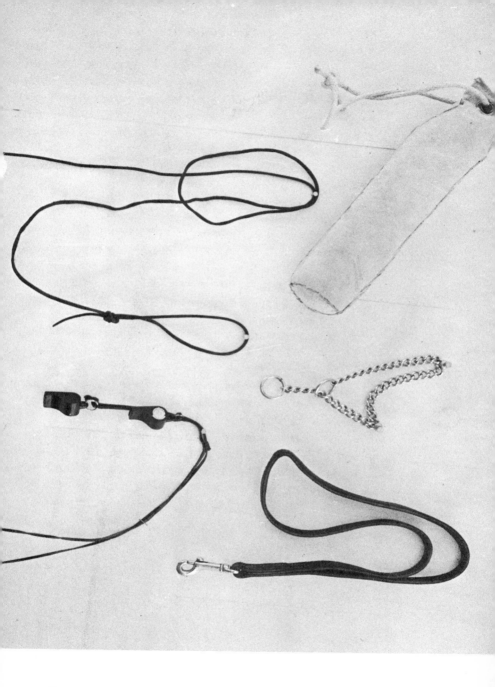

*Some necessary equipment. Clockwise from the upper left: Train-
ing Dummy, Choke Collar, Leash, Whistles, Belt Cord.*

SIT " . . . up on the leash as you press down with the other hand."

STAY "... back ... away from your dog repeating 'Stay' as you do so."

COME." ... a series of quick jerks will prove more effective than will a long tug-

HEEL " . . . walk forward and urge your dog to 'heel.'"

13

KENNEL " . . . open the run, or crate, door and tell him to 'kennel.' "

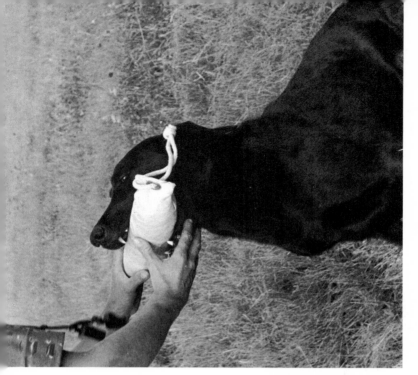

THE TRAINING DUMMY ". . . prevent him from dropping it. Remember, he must learn to hold the training dummy until commanded to "drop it."

15

". . . shake his head and command him to "stop that noise.""

Land Double with Honoring: Low Stubble

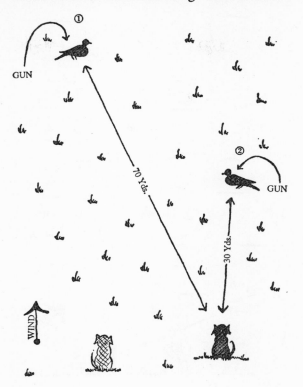

This is not a difficult test and is included here only for the purpose of illustrating the honoring dog. The AKC "Standard Procedure for Nonslip Retriever Trials" states: "In at least one series in all stakes, except Derby, every dog should be kept on line off leash while another dog works." (See also *Honor* in glossary.)

Water Double with Honoring: Wading—Swimming Reeds

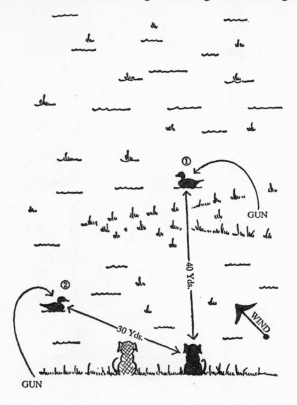

Here again we encounter the honoring dog. Normally dogs are required to honor on land, but it is wise to prepare for the possibility of honoring on a water test. The test itself is not too difficult, although many dogs are apt to hunt the long, right-hand bird short. Failing this, they are apt to hunt out the point of land where the guns are stationed. Depth perception is all-important here.

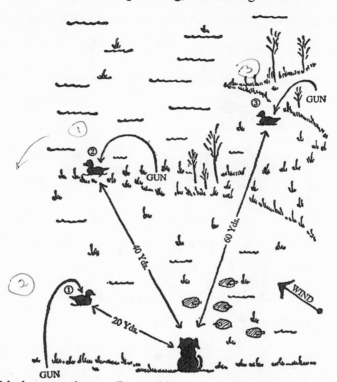

This is a tough test. It would be a tough test in an Open Stake and is just that much tougher as a Qualifying test. The placement of the birds is normal for a hard triple; it is the order in which they are thrown that makes it very difficult. A dog that has been trained to take the last bird first is in more trouble than one that takes the short bird first, but in either case there are still two ducks to pick up. Let us assume that the dog has picked up the far bird first. He will then, in all but very rare instances, pick up the short bird next. The dog taking the short bird first will undoubtedly take the far bird next, as it is the one he remembers most vividly. Each dog has now picked up both the left- and right-hand birds. There remains for each to retrieve the number two, or middle, duck. Are they in trouble? It is enough to say that no dog will be able to pick up the bird without a great deal of handling. This actually is not surprising. Dogs learn only by doing, and they learned to do triples the other way round. This is not a test you can train for with a young dog, but it does illustrate the importance of mixing up the order of the falls now and then.

Land Blind: Weeds and Green Corn

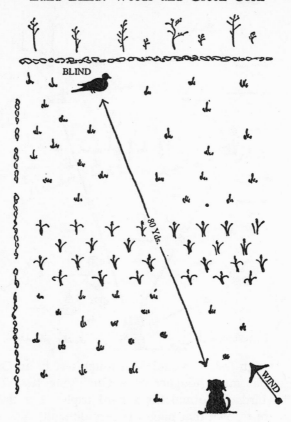

This is not a hard blind, nor is it a long one. However, it has a hazard that all too few people train against. If a dog is to complete this blind retrieve in good form he must take a line through the standing corn without deviating from said line. Once beyond the corn he can be handled to the bird with comparative ease. Many dogs do not believe that the bird can be anywhere but in the tempting cover and decide that this is where the bird is to be found, despite their handler's directions to the contrary. This is a test it would be wise to train for; any standing cover with an open area beyond will serve as well as does the corn.

Land and Water Blind: Marsh with Ditches

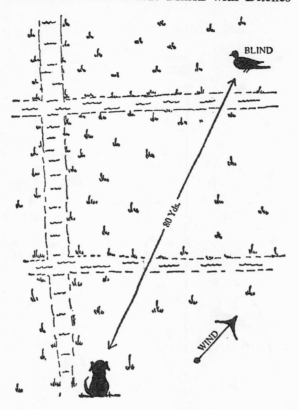

This is another relatively easy blind, but few young dogs are apt to do it without a certain amount of difficulty. The dog that holds a line here is unusual. The ditches coupled with the fact that the dog is approaching each at an angle, present hazards that the dog is apt to avoid. His tendency will be to fade with the wind and run along the near side of each, crossing only when stopped and handled. This is an often-encountered type of test and one that needs practice.

Land Double and Blind: Stubble

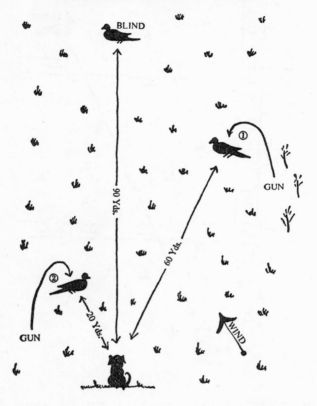

This is not a particularly hard test. Few dogs are apt to have any predictable trouble with the marked birds, but it is these same birds that create the hazards for the blind. Many dogs will want to return to area of one fall or the other en route to the blind. This is a test you will see quite often and one that is worthy of practice.

Water Double-Double: Marsh, Swimming Water—Tall Reeds

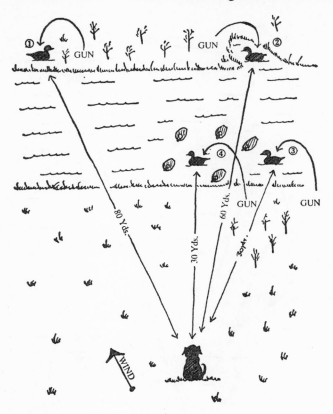

This is a tricky test and one that requires a long memory on the part of any dog. The test goes this way: The two long falls are thrown in order, left and right. The handler is told to get the right-hand bird first, which then is accomplished with little or no difficulty; at this time the number three and four birds are thrown into the decoys. These are also retrieved with only minor difficulties. Now the money bird remains to be retrieved; needless to say, a great many dogs have to be handled to this. Although this is not a test you will encounter often, it is well to practice tests of this type occasionally.

Water Triple: Marsh—Swimming, Wading Water

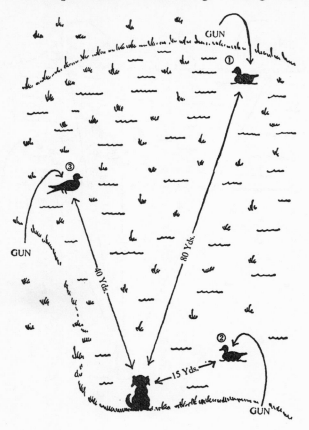

This is not a particularly difficult triple. It is pictured here for the purpose of illustrating a triple that utilizes more than one type of game bird. This is work that is well worth training your dog for, whether you have trials or that dreamed-of double on woodcock and partridge as your incentive.

Water Blind and Diversion: Swimming Water

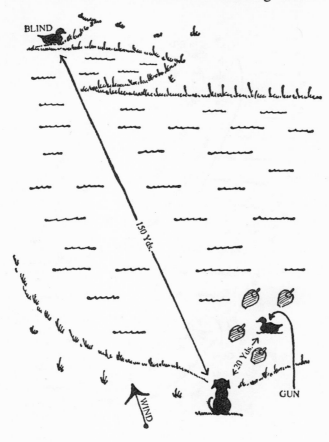

On paper this looks easy, but how often do you train your dog to do blinds across one hundred and fifty yards of open water? Here again is a test that you will not often encounter, but one that is easily prepared for. A further complication here is that a dog having become convinced that you really do want him to go way out there will in nine out of ten cases go ashore at the first available place. Will your retriever respond to directions at that distance?

Channel Blind with Diversion: Swimming Water, High Banks

This test is just as it looks: a short bird that some dogs will run the bank to retrieve and a long channel blind. The judges' instructions are to keep your dog in the water en route to the blind. There is only one way to be prepared for a channel blind and that is to practice, practice and practice.

Land Blind and Diversion: Low Stubble

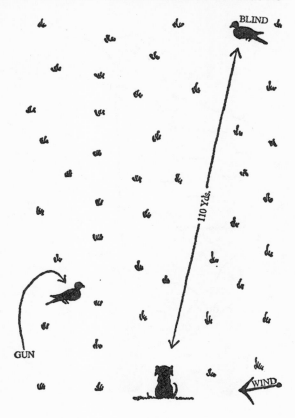

This is not a tough test, but it is one that many of the more competent, older dogs will line to without a whistle. It is therefore up to you to put distractions in the path of your dog in your training sessions. In this way your dog will soon learn that old falls are just that and that you know a good deal more about the location of the next bird than he does.

Water Quadruple: Brush, Reeds and Swimming Water

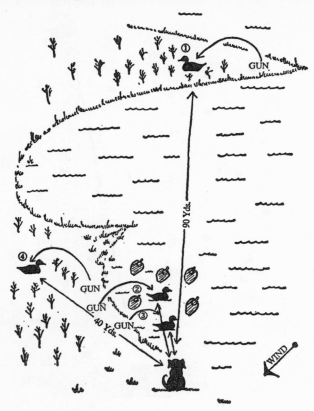

While this is obviously a complicated test, it is not a particularly difficult one. The test goes something like this: long bird on the point, two birds in the decoys, and a flyer shot in the woods. Though not often encountered, here again is a test that would be advisable to train on from time to time, especially if your dog has no trouble counting to three.

Land Double with Honoring: Weeds and Corn

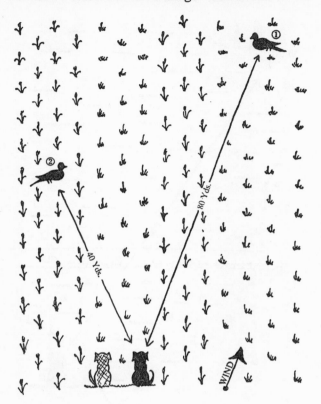

The hazard in this test is rather obvious—the open cover between the two plantings of corn. Even though a dog has no trouble with the left bird, which is not necessarily assured, the tendency is to hunt the corn rather than the open cover for the second bird. Here again is a test that is often encountered, and one that it is well to be prepared for.

Land and Water Blind: Bank, Marsh, Road, Swimming Water

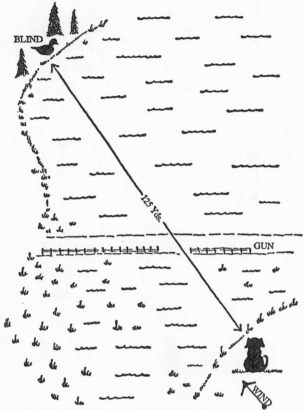

This is primarily a water blind, but one in which the major hazard is represented by a land area. On paper the test does not look too complex, but in reality it is one that only the most experienced dogs will be able to complete. A shot is fired, but the dog sees nothing; he is then sent for the blind. The route is through the water immediately in front of the dog, to and through the opening in the fence, across the road and into the water en route to the far shore. If you do not feel that this is a most difficult test, try it. It is not necessary to have your dog trained for this extreme-type blind, but it would be well to set up some work that will make it necessary for him to cross land and then re-enter the water en route to a blind.

Water Triple: Swimming Water, High Reeds

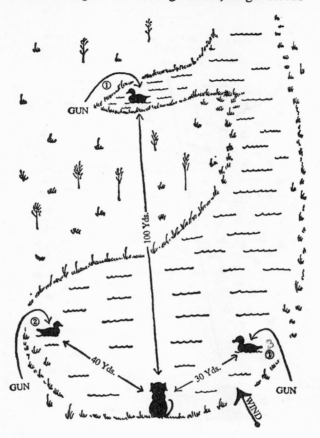

This test presents the same general hazard that was encountered in the last test—land en route to water. Few dogs will have trouble with the first two, short birds, but they will in all likelihood encounter some difficulty in retrieving the long duck. Dogs swimming across the bay will tend either to lose their line, or hunt out the land area. In either case they are very apt to have a long hunt for the far bird. Dogs running either bank will have even greater difficulties. In short, the long bird is a hard fall—one that requires not only a near-perfect line, but also a great sense of depth perception.

Water Blind: Marsh, Swimming Water

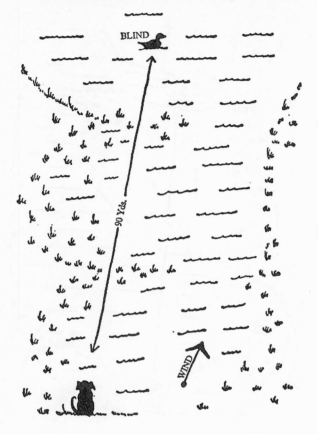

This, while not a particularly difficult blind, illustrates a test that many dogs will have trouble with. The hazards lie in the fact that the dog having been sent for the blind is either going to hold a good line through the first point of cover or be out of sight and subsequently out of control; he must then cross the open water and repeat the hazardous crossing at the second point. In each case many dogs will want to hunt the cover rather than go into open water where they can see nothing to interest them. This is a test of both line and control, and one that is well worth training on.

Double Land Blind: Low Stubble

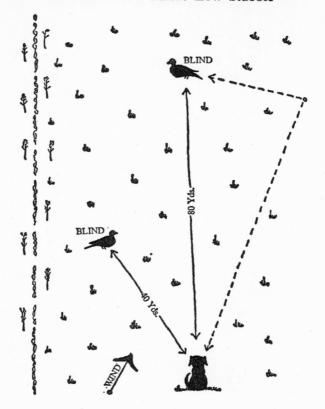

This would be easy if you could do it the obvious way, but the Judges' instructions are: "Get the long bird first." There is only one way to accomplish this and that is to send your dog on a line that will make it impossible to wind the short bird before he winds the long one. (See dotted line on diagram.) This is a test that requires your dog to take, and hold, the initial line; in short, it is a test that requires complete control. While this is not a test you will often encounter, it is one that will enable you to achieve a great degree of control, one that will be well worth working on.

VIII

Judging Your Retriever

Whether or not you have an interest in retriever trials you should put your retriever's abilities to the test. It matters not whether Judges or you yourself evaluate your retriever, the end conclusions will be the same. Gundog or field trial prospect, any well-trained retriever should be able to complete the tests included in this chapter.

If you set up intelligent tests in the training of your dog and then keep a record of his work on each test, you will be well on your way to an honest evaluation of your retriever. Anyone, whether he be interested in field trials or not, should be interested in perfecting the working ability of his dog. A program of tests with record keeping will show up minor faults before they become serious.

The eight tests included here are carefully diagrammed with location of and distance to each fall, direction of wind, the varying terrain and its resulting hazards indicated. In addition, the work as actually accomplished by four different retrievers is shown and discussed. All in all, this chapter is intended to enable you to judge and evaluate your own retriever.

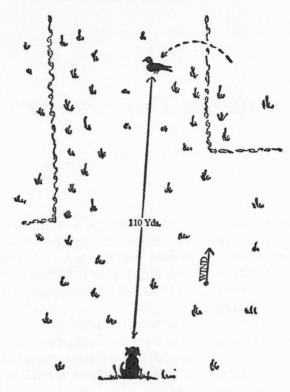

110 Yds.

WIND

This is not a difficult test, in fact, it is relatively simple. The hazards are the rather dense corners en route to the bird. All but one dog was pulled to one or both of these corners. This is an easy test to set up and one that deserves your time and attention.

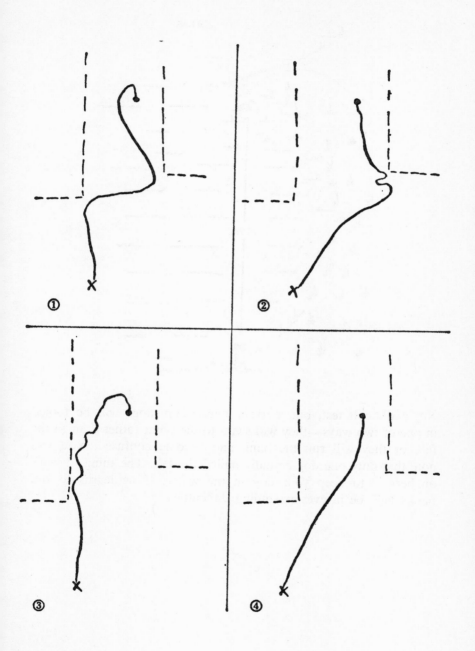

① ② ③ ④

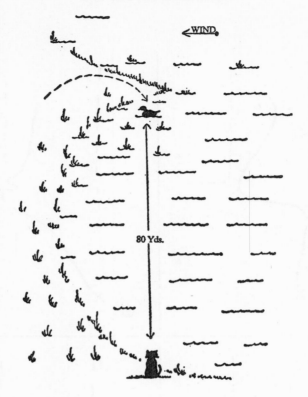

Not a difficult test, but a tricky one. Many dogs will be fooled in one of two ways—they will swim to the point rather than to the fall, or they will run the bank and become confused. You will note that only one dog actually nailed the fall. The thing to work on here is to keep your dog in the water. If he learns to run banks he'll be in ever-expanding difficulties.

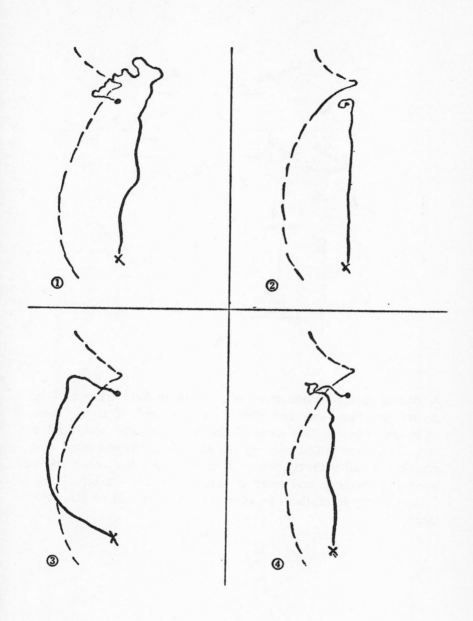

A double that is encountered often both in field trials and in normal shooting—one that should be practiced. You will note from the diagrams that none of the dogs had any real trouble here. Two were pulled back by the short fall, but recovered and got the far fall without great difficulties. The other two showed a positive memory and more or less nailed the far bird. Easy though it may seem, this type of water double should be practiced often.

The 1961 National Amateur Champion, Ace's Sheba of Arden,
owned by Mr. & Mrs. William K. Laughlin

For blind retrieves you must teach your dog the hand signals on the following pages. Start with GET BACK *as shown above, and concentrate on it until the signal has been mastered by the dog.*

The second hand signal: GET OVER *RIGHT. As with* GET BACK *blow one whistle blast to attract the dog's attention and then give the signal to* GET OVER.

The third hand signal: GET OVER *LEFT. Confine your training to one hand signal a day.*

The fourth hand signal: COME IN. *An easily mastered signal once the first three have been learned. The dog is already familiar with the whistled signal to "come."*

After your dog has mastered the basic hand signals he is ready
to learn to take a line from your side to a fall he has not seen.

WATER RETRIEVES. *"Some dogs will break ice to swim."*
Mandy at three months takes to water like a fish.

"It won't take him long to learn proper bird handling. . . ." A young Golden handles a pigeon in the proper way. This dog went on to become one of the top amateur trained and handled retrievers in the country. Amateur Field Champion, Happy Thanksgiving C.D., owned by Ann Fowler.

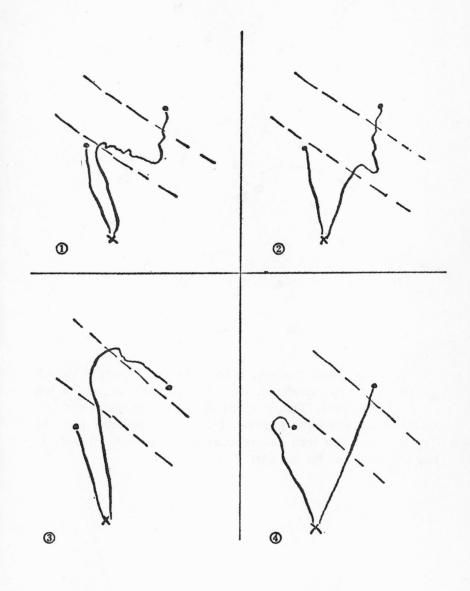

① ② ③ ④

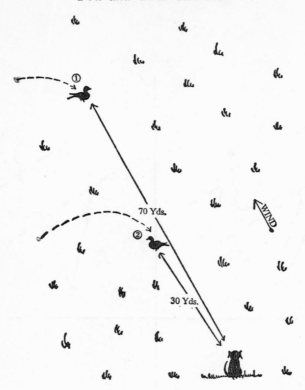

This is not a simple test—no in-line double is. Some dogs will become completely confused, some just partially so, and a few will nail both birds. This is a test of depth perception and will need practice and more practice. The average retriever picks up the short bird and then has difficulty in going back on more or less the same line for the next. Try it and see.

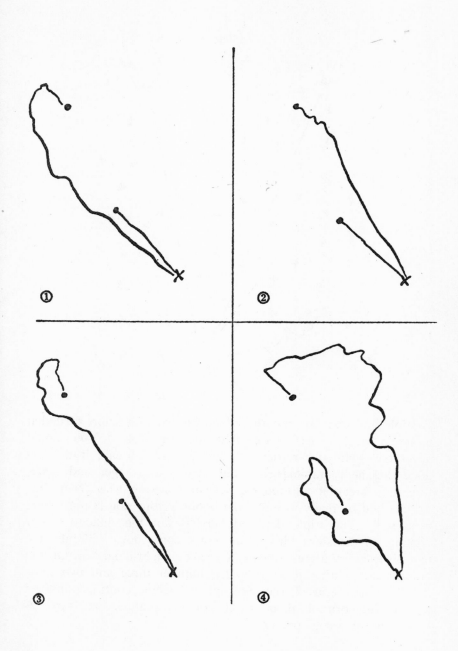

① ② ③ ④

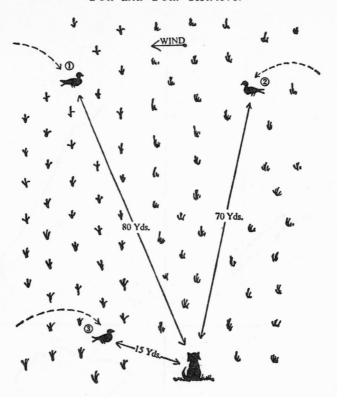

A triple and one that has the added hazard of a short bird that is a real breaking test. (Note that one dog broke.) You should never feel that your retriever is not going to break; if he is a good dog he is automatically high-strung and eager and therefore may break if allowed to. Set up breaking tests from time to time and be ready to lower the boom if your dog is not steady as a rock. The triple depicted here is not too difficult. After picking up the short bird in the corn, some dogs will take the first bird next and consequently forget the right-hand fall. On the other hand, if after picking up the number three and two birds they become confused, they are apt to become confused and get lost in the corn on their search for the number one bird. A good type of test to practice.

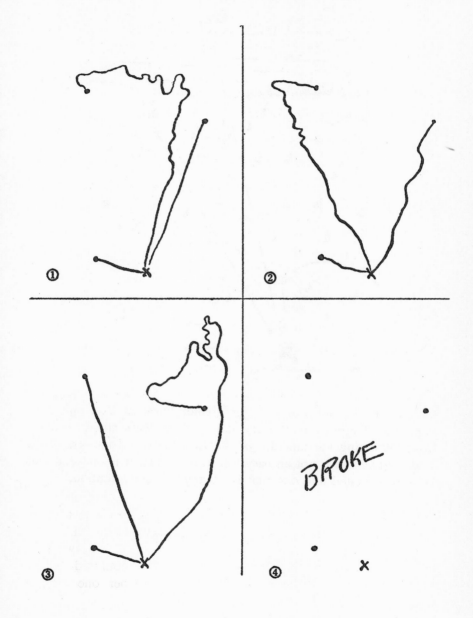

① ② ③ ④ BROKE

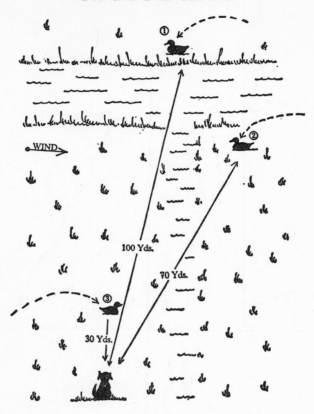

Another triple, but one with far greater hazards. You will note from the diagrams that every dog had at least slight troubles in encountering the juncture of the two channels, one with both birds. While this is not an easy test to duplicate, it is one that can be approximated and one that is worthy of your attention.

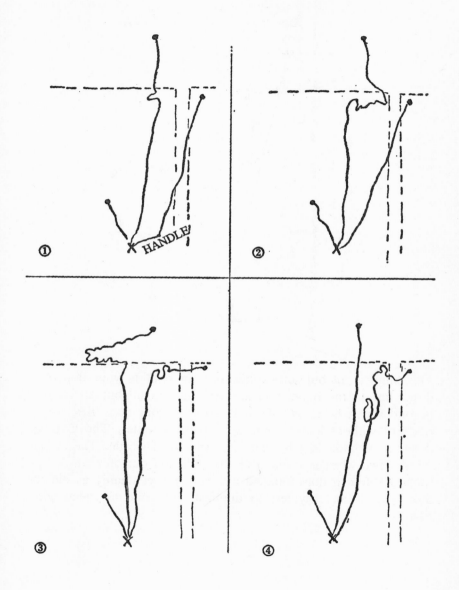

① HANDLE ② ③ ④

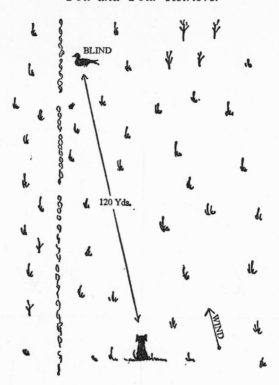

This blind is all but self-explanatory. In sending your dog on a direct line to the blind, you are sending him all but at the wall beyond which he is out of sight. To send your dog on a line to the bird without losing control is no easy matter. The first dog did a commendable job, requiring only one whistle. The second refused two whistles, went over the wall and out of control. The third and fourth dogs handled well but not as cleanly as did the first. This is an easy test to duplicate and one to spend some time on.

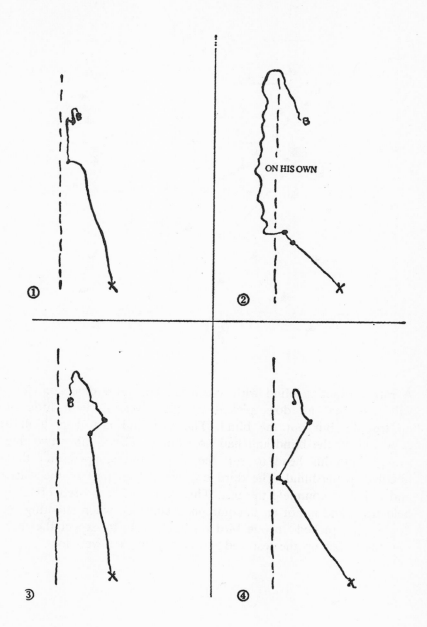

① ② ON HIS OWN ③ ④

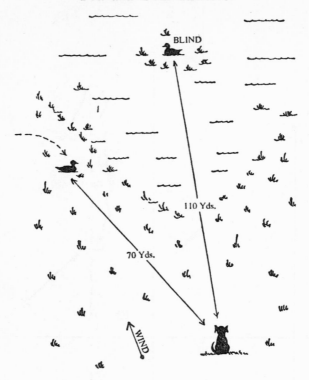

A rather exacting blind with a marked bird as a diversion. You will note that all dogs picked up the diversion with little or no trouble, but not the blind. The first and last dogs took a good line to the blind and had no trouble. The number two dog took it into his head to run the shore, but stopped and then handled to the blind. The third dog wanted no part of the water and failed to complete the test. This type of test is used often in field trials and is not an uncommon occurrence when shooting. A dog having picked up one bird on land tends to expect the next one there. Set up the test and see how your retriever does.

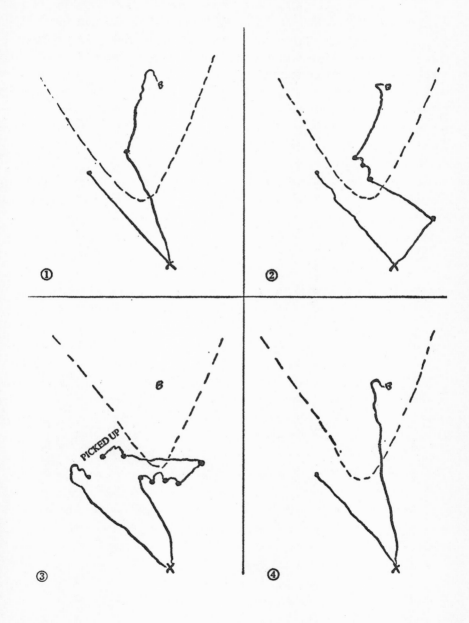

① ② ③ ④

PICKED UP

The foregoing tests and discussions are included here to help you honestly judge and evaluate your retriever. A program of training that does not include a fair appraisal of the end results is rather worthless. Train your retriever, judge and evaluate his work and then correct his faults; in this way your retriever will be on the road to perfection.

Conclusion

This book has attempted to help *you* train *your* retriever. However, there is a group of heretofore unmentioned people, the professional trainers and handlers, who are the real experts and the people to whom you should turn for assistance should you be unable to train your own retriever

Whether they are trained by professionals or amateurs, retrievers will be hunted over and run in field trials for many years to come. In a duck blind or at a field trial, the best of luck to you and your retriever.

RWC, Jr.

Appendix

Standards of the Breed

Labrador Retriever—Standard of the Breed

GENERAL APPEARANCE

The general appearance of the Labrador should be that of a strongly built, short-coupled, very active dog. He should be fairly wide over the loins, and strong and muscular in the hindquarters. The coat should be close, short, dense and free from feather.

DETAILED DESCRIPTION

Head: The skull should be wide, giving brain room; there should be a slight "stop," i.e., the brow should be slightly pronounced, so that the skull is not absolutely in a straight line with the nose. The head should be clean-cut and free from fleshy cheeks. The jaws should be long and powerful and free from snipiness; the nose should be wide and the nostrils well developed. Teeth should be strong and regular, with a level mouth.

The ears should hang moderately close to the head, rather far back, should be set somewhat low and not large and heavy. The eyes should be of medium size, expressing great intelligence and a good temper, can be brown, yellow or black, but brown or black is preferred.

Neck and Chest: The neck should be medium length and powerful and not throaty. The shoulders should be long and sloping.

The chest must be of good width and depth, the ribs well sprung and the loins wide and strong, stifles well turned, and the hindquarters well developed and of great power.

Legs and Feet: The legs must be straight from the shoulder to ground, and the feet compact with toes well arched, the pads well developed; the hocks should be well bent, and the dog must neither be cow-hocked nor too wide behind; in fact, he must stand and move true all round on legs and feet. Legs should be of medium length, show-ing good bone and muscle, but not so short as to be out of balance with the rest of body. In fact, a dog well balanced in all points is preferable to one with outstanding good qualities and defects.

Tail: The tail is a distinctive feature of the breed: it should be very thick toward the base, gradually tapering toward the tip, of medium length, should be free from any feathering, and should be clothed thickly all round with the Labrador's short, thick, dense coat, thus giving the particular "rounded" appearance that has been described as the "otter" tail. The tail may be carried gaily but should not curl over the back.

Coat: The coat is another very distinctive feature; it should be short, very dense and without wave, and should give a fairly hard feel-ing to the hand.

Color: The colors are black, yellow, or chocolate and are evaluated as follows:

(a) Blacks: All black, with a small white spot on chest permis-sible. Eyes to be of medium size, expressing intelligence and good temper, preferably brown or hazel, although black or yellow is per-missible.

(b) Yellows: Yellows may vary in color from fox-red to light cream with variations in the shading of the coat on ears, the under-parts of the dog, or beneath the tail. A small white spot on chest is permissible. Eye coloring and expression should be the same as that of the blacks, with black or dark brown eye rims. The nose should also be black or dark brown, although "fading" to pink in winter weather is not serious. A "Dudley" nose (pink without pigmentation) should be penalized.

(c) Chocolates: Shades ranging from light sedge to chocolate. A small white spot on chest is permissible. Eyes to be light brown to clear yellow. Nose and eye rim pigmentation dark brown or liver col-ored. "Fading" to pink in winter weather not serious. "Dudley" nose should be penalized.

Movement: Movement should be free and effortless. The forelegs should be strong, straight and true, and correctly placed. Watching a dog move toward one, there should be no signs of elbows being out in front, but they should be neatly held to the body with legs not too close together and moving straight forward without pacing or weav-ing. Upon viewing the dog from the rear, one should get the impression that the hind legs, which should be well muscled and not cow-hocked, move as nearly parallel, with hocks doing their full share of work and flexing well, thus giving the appearance of power and strength.

Approximate weight of dogs and bitches in working condition:

Dogs:	60 to 75 lbs.
Bitches:	55 to 70 lbs.

Height at shoulders:

Dogs:	22½ inches to 24½ inches
Bitches:	21½ inches to 23½ inches

Golden Retriever—Standard of the Breed

A symmetrical, powerful, active dog, sound and well put together, not clumsy or long in the leg, displaying a kindly expression and possessing a personality that is eager, alert and self-confident. Primarily a hunting dog, he should be shown in hardworking condition. Overall appearance, balance, gait and purpose to be given more emphasis than his component parts.

Size—Males 23–24 inches in height at withers; females 21½–22½. Length from breastbone to buttocks slightly greater than height at withers in ratio of 12 to 11. Weight for dogs 65–75 pounds; bitches 60–70 pounds.

Head—Broad in skull, slightly arched laterally and longitudinally without prominence of frontal or occipital bones. Good stop. Foreface deep and wide, nearly as long as skull. Muzzle, when viewed in profile, slightly deeper at stop than at tip; when viewed from above, slightly wider at stop than at tip. No heaviness in flews. Removal of whiskers for show purposes optional. *Eyes*—Friendly and intelligent, medium large with dark rims, set well apart and reasonably deep in sockets. Color preferably dark brown, never lighter than color of coat. No white or haw visible when looking straight ahead. *Teeth*—Scissors bite with lower incisors touching inside of upper incisors. *Nose*—Black or dark brown, though lighter shade in cold weather not serious. Dudley nose (pink without pigmentation) to be faulted. *Ears*—Rather short, hanging flat against head with rounded tips slightly below jaw. Forward edge attached well behind and just above eye with rear edge slightly below eye. Low, houndlike ear-set to be faulted.

Neck—Medium long, sloping well back into shoulders, giving sturdy muscular appearance with untrimmed natural ruff. No throatiness.

Body—Well balanced, short-coupled, deep through the heart. Chest at least as wide as a man's hand, including thumb. Brisket extends to elbows. Ribs long and well sprung, but not barrel shaped, extending well to rear of body. Loin short, muscular, wide and deep, with very little tuck-up. Topline level from withers to croup, whether standing or moving. Croup slopes gently. Slabsidedness, narrow chest, lack of depth in brisket, excessive tuck-up, roach- or swayback to be faulted.

Forequarters—Forequarters well coordinated with hindquarters and capable of free movement. Shoulder blades wide, long and muscular, showing angulation with upper arm of approximately 90 degrees. Legs straight with good bone. Pastern short and strong, sloping slightly forward with no suggestion of weakness.

Hindquarters—Well-bent stifles (angle between femur and pelvis approximately 90 degrees) with hocks well let down. Legs straight when viewed from rear. Cow hocks and sickle hocks to be faulted.

Feet—Medium size, round and compact with thick pads. Excess hair may be trimmed to show natural size and contour. Open or splayed feet to be faulted. *Tail*—Well set on, neither too high nor too low, following natural line of croup. Length extends to hock. Carried with merry action with some upward curve but never curled over back or between legs.

Coat and color—Dense and water-repellent with good undercoat. Texture not as hard as that of a short-haired dog or as silky as that of a setter. Lies flat against body and may be straight or wavy. Moderate feathering on back of forelegs and heavier feathering on front of neck, back of thighs and underside of tail. Feathering may be lighter than rest of coat. Color lustrous golden of various shades. A few white hairs on chest permissible but not desirable. Further white markings to be faulted.

Gait—When trotting, gait is free, smooth, powerful and well coordinated. Viewed from front or rear, legs turn neither in nor out, nor do feet cross or interfere with each other. Increased speed causes tendency of feet to converge toward center line of gravity.

DISQUALIFICATIONS

Deviation in height of more than one inch from the standard either way. Undershot or overshot jaws—not to be confused with misalignment of teeth. Trichiasis—abnormal position or direction of the eyelashes.

Chesapeake Bay Retriever—Standard of the Breed

Head—Skull, broad and round with medium stop; nose, medium-short muzzle, pointed but not sharp. Lips thin, not pendulous. Ears small, set well up on head, hanging loosely and of medium leather. Eyes medium-large, very clear, of yellowish color and wide apart. *Neck*— Of medium length with a strong muscular appearance, tapering to shoulders.

Shoulders, Chest and Body—Shoulders: sloping and should have full liberty of action with plenty of power without restrictions of movement. Chest: strong, deep and wide; barrel round and deep. Body: of medium length, neither cobbled nor roached, but rather approaching hollowness, flanks well tucked up. *Back Quarters and Stiffles*—Back quarters should be as high or a trifle higher than the shoulders. They should show fully as much power as the forequarters. There should be no tendency to weakness in either fore- or hindquarters. Hindquarters should be especially powerful to supply the driving power for swimming. Back should be short, well-coupled and powerful. Good hindquarters are essential.

Legs, Elbows, Hocks and Feet—Legs should be medium-length and straight, showing good bone and muscle, with well-webbed hare feet of good size. The toes well rounded and close, pasterns and hocks medium length. The straighter the legs the better.

Stern—Tail should be medium-length, varying from: 12 to 15 inches for males, and 11 to 14 inches for females. Medium-heavy at base. Moderate feathering on stern and tail permissible.

Coat and Texture—Coat should be thick and short, nowhere over 1½ inches long, with a dense fine woolly undercoat. Hair on face and legs should be very short and straight with tendency to wave on the shoulders, neck, back and loin only. The curly coat or coat with a tendency to curl not permissible. *Color*—Any color varying from a dark brown to a faded tan or deadgrass. Deadgrass takes in any shade of deadgrass, from a tan to a deep straw color. White spot on breast and toes permissible, but the smaller the spot the better. Solid color is preferred.

Weight—Males, 65 to 75 pounds; females 55 to 65 pounds.

Height—Males 23 to 26 inches; females 21 to 24 inches.

Symmetry and Quality—The Chesapeake dog should show a bright and happy disposition and an intelligent expression, with general outlines impressive and denoting a good worker. The dog should be well proportioned—a dog with a good coat and well balanced in points being preferable to the dog excelling in some points but weak in others.

The texture of the dog's coat is very important, as the dog is used for hunting under all sorts of adverse weather conditions, often working in ice and snow. The oil in the harsh outer coat and woolly under-coat is of extreme value in preventing the cold water from reaching the dog's skin and aids in quick drying. A Chesapeake's coat should resist water in the same way that a duck's feathers do. When he leaves the water and shakes himself, his coat should not hold the water at all, being merely moist. Color and coat are extremely important, as the dog is used for duck hunting. The color must be as nearly that of his surroundings as possible; also, dogs are exposed to all kinds of adverse weather conditions, often working in ice and snow. So the color and the texture of coat must be given every consideration when judging on the bench or in the ring.

Courage, willingness to work, alertness, nose, intelligence, love of water, general quality, and, most of all, disposition should be given primary consideration in the selection and breeding of the Chesapeake Bay dog.

POSITIVE SCALE OF POINTS

Head, incl. lips, ears and eyes	16
Neck	4
Shoulders and body	12
Back quarters and stiffles	12
Elbows, legs and feet	12
Color	4
Stern and tail	10
Coat and texture	18
General conformation	12
Total	100

Note—The question of coat and general type of balance takes precedence over any scoring table that could be drawn up.

APPROXIMATE MEASUREMENTS

	Inches
Length head, nose to occiput	9½ to 10
Girth at ears	20 to 21
Muzzle below eyes	10 to 10½
Length of ears	4½ to 5
Width between eyes	2½ to 2¾
Girth neck close to shoulder	20 to 22

Girth of chest to elbows	35	to 36
Girth at flank	24	to 25
Girth forearms at shoulders	10	to 10½
Length from occiput to tail base	34	to 35
Girth upper thigh	19	to 20
From root to root of ear, over skull	5	to 6
Occiput to top of shoulder blades	9	to 9½
From elbow to elbow over the shoulders	25	to 26

DISQUALIFICATIONS

Black or liver-colored. White on any part of body, except breast or belly or spots on feet. Feathering on tail or legs over 1¾ inches long. Dewclaws, undershot or any deformity. Coat curly or tendency to curl all over body. Specimens unworthy or lacking in breed characteristics.

List of Field and Amateur Field Trial Champions

LABRADOR RETRIEVERS

Ace High Scamp of Windswept
Ace's Dike of Winniway
Ace's Sheba of Arden
Ace's Storm of Winniway
Alpine Cherokee Rocket
Ar-dee Smorgasbord
Arden's Ace of Merwalfin
Avalanche Burnt Sage
Aztec Chips
Bakewell Donder
Ballyduff Jester
Banchory Night Light of Wingan
Banchory Varnish of Wingan
Bay City Zany Jane
Beau Brummel of Wyndale
Beau of The Lark
Beau of Zenith
Beautywoods Carbon Copy
Beautywoods Peggydidit
Beautywoods Sooty Scamp
Beavercreek Bandit
Belle of Zenith
Bengal of Arden
Bigstone Bandit
Bigstone Demon of Bruce
Bigstone Hope
Bingo's Ringo
Bing's Tar Baby
Bitterroot Chink-ee
Black Boy XI
Black Brook's Lady Bimba
Black Brook's Miss Chief
Black Corsair of Whitmore

Black Cougar
Black Dusky
Black Jet XVI
Black Magic of Audlon
Black Monk of Roeland
Black Panther
Black Point Dark Destroyer
Black Point Rising Sun
Black Point Sweep's Chance
Black Prince of Sag Harbor
Black Roland of Koshkonong
Blind of Arden
Blitzen Nick
Blitzen II
Boar Ranch Nip
Bob Speed
Boise Buckeroo
Boley's Cascade
Boley's Tar Baby
Bracken's Flash
Bracken's High Flyer
Bracken's Sweep
Braes of Arden
Brignall's Fleet
Brignall's Gringo
Brignall's Nick
Buffington of Yellowstone
Burnham Buff
Butch's Bitterroot Smokey
Canuck Stealer
Carbon of Barrington
Carity's Smudge
Carity's Timer of Black Wolf

Carr-Lab Hilltop
Cherokee Buck
Cherokee Medicine Man
Chevriers Golden Rod
Chino Bacchus
Cindie of Salomonson
Cindy's Pride of Garfield
Clear Weather
Cliff's Patrick
Cork of Oakwood Lane
Count of Garfield
Dacity's Black Spider
Dairy Hill's Night Cap
Dairy Hill's Night Watch
Dairy Hill's Tart
Dandy Dan of Repman
Dan McGrew of Wake
Decoy of Arden
Deer Creek's Bewise
Deer Creek's Cforcatl
Della-Winns Tar of Craignook
Del-Tone Colvin
Del-Tone Ric
Di Mondi's Danny
Discovery of Franklin
Dolobran's Angus
Dolobran's Little Ash
Dolobran's Smoke Tail
Dolobran's Spook
Dolobran's Streak
Duke of Ashton
Ebony Babe of Jolor
Ebony's Jet Rebel
El-Jay's Ace Scenter
El-Jay's Smokey Willow War
Farbee's Dugan
Firelei of Deer Creek
Firelei's Hornet
Frances Fishtail
Freehaven Again
Freehaven Jay
Freehaven Muscles
Gabriel of Cram

Gilmore's Peggy
Glenairlie Rocket
Glenairlie Rover
Glengarvin's Kim
Go-Kits Gypsy
Gordy's Black Boy
Gorse of Arden
Grangemead Precious
Gun of Arden
Hal's Spy-Wise Zeke
Havenhurst Cliffspride
Hello Joe of Rocheltree
Hightail of Wyandotte
Hiwood Fleet
Hiwood Mike
Hiwood My Delight
Hiwood Storm
Honey Chile Trixie
Hot Coffee of Random Lake
Howies Happy Hunter
Hurricane's Don Juan
Ila's Black Joe
Invail's Pennell
Jack Pot's Second Whirl
Jet IV
Jet of Sugar Valley
Jet of Zenith
Jibodad Gypsy
Jibodad Topper
Jibodad Velvet
Jiggaboo of Mountaindale
Jolor's Amigo
Jolor's Snapshot
Jupiter of Avondale
Keith's Black Atom
Keith's Black Magic
Kilsyth Cleo
Kimbow General Ike
King Buck
Kingswere Black Ebony
Knight Rider
Koko Clipper Dipper
Krooked Kreek Jupiter J.

Ladies Day at Deer Creek
La Sage's Neb
La Sage's Smokey
Ledgeland's Dora
Little Magic Lady
Little Miss Timber
Lone Star Blackie
Lucinda of Crater Lake
Maidscorner Paul
Mainliner Mike
Major VI
Major Tobin of Island Acres
Malarkey's Okanagon Pat
Manazel Clover
Manazel Nimbus
Marion's Timothy
Markwell's Ramblin Rebel
Marten's Little Bullet
Marvadel Black Gum
Mary-Go-Round Deer Creek
Massie's Sassy Boots
Matchmaker for Deer Creek
Meadow Farm Night
Medlin's Texas Right
Michael of Lakeview
Ming
Miss Madison
Mr. Jic of Maryglo
Mr. Jones of Nishayuna
Mitzee's Chipper
Mott Place Captain
Mully Gully Goo
Nelgard's Counterpoint
Nic O Bet's Black Candy
Nigger of Barrington
Nigger of Swinomish
Nig's Black Phantom
Nilo Buck Tail Buck
Nilo Possibility
Nilo Senator
Nilo's Solo Margie
Noah of Swinomish
Nodak Ar-Dee

Nodak Boots
Orchardton Dale
Orchardton Dorando
Paha Sapa Belle
Paha Sapa Chief
Paha Sapa War Cloud
Peconic Pyne of Arden
Penny Girl
Pepper's Jiggs
Pickpocket of Deer Creek
Pinehawk Black Tarquin of Glaven
Pinehawk Nigger
Pinocchio of Maryglo
Pitch of Timer Trouble
Prairie Smoke
Princess Black Belle
Princess Patricia Stieg
Queenie of Redding
Rick of Charlemagne
Rick of Craignook
Riefler's Dutch
Rinney's Cumulo Nimbus
Ripco's Peter Pan
Rip of Holly Hill
Rip of Wake
Rip's Bingo
Roy's Rowdy
Salt Valley Ottie
Salty of Sugar Valley
Sam Frizel of Glenspey
Sam of Alaska
Sandbar Pete
Sand Gold Terry
Scoronine of Deer Creek
Sentinel of Whitmore
Shadow's Ebony Bob
Shauna Buck
Shed of Arden
Shed's Dinah of Whitefish
Shed's Prince of Garfield
Shoremeadow Tidewater
Sir Jock
Slo-Poke Smokey of Dairy Hill

"... a dog whose purpose it is to retrieve fallen game."

Correctly introduce your dog to a boat and he'll beat you to it every chance he gets.

On a hunting trip give careful attention to the needs and comfort of your retriever.

27

Take care when rigging your decoys. Short lines and separate riggings will be more time-consuming, but also dog-saving.

This is what he was trained for.

At a field trial, the best shots in the area are asked to shoot.

A great field trial competitor, King Buck, the 1952–53 National Champion.

A field trial is not only an excellent opportunity to test the ability of the dog, but also the handler.

At a field trial, the Judges are called upon to set up fair, yet exacting tests.

Smudge's Bingo
Snake River Dilly
Speed of Lancaster
Spirit Lake Bay
Spirit Lake Duke
Spirit Lake Phantom
Sprig of Swinomish
Staindrop Kim
Staindrop Murton Marksman
Staindrop Ringleader
Staindrop Spanker
Staindrop Striker
Stan's Curly Boy
Star of Fate
Stonegate's Ace of Spades
Stonegate's Black Diamond
Strawberry Hill Regent
Sumpawam's Tide Rip
Sungo
Swifty of Sugar Valley
Tanca's Rocky of Random Lake
Tan O Shanter of Craignook
Tar Baby of Holly Hill
Tar Baby's Little Sweet Stuff
Tarblood of Abrasaka

Tar of Arden
Teal Tammy of Glago
Techacko's Ranger
The Spider of Kingswere
The Web of Kingswere
Timber Town Clansman
Toto of Audlon
Trabington's Black Witch
Treveilyr Swift
Tri-Strada Gun Moll
Truly Yours of Garfield
Tyson Rowdy
Webway's Crusader
West Island Chief
West Island Comet
West Island Raven
West Island Tramp
West Island Whiz
Woodcroft Inga's Bonus
Yankee Clipper of Reo Raj
Yodel of Morexpense
Young Mint of Catawba
Zip
Zipper of Sugar Valley

GOLDEN RETRIEVERS

April Showers
Banty of Woodend
Beauty of Sunburg
Beautywoods Tamarack
Brandy Snifter
Brigg's Lake Mac
Commanche Cayenne
Craigmar Dustrack
Cresta Chip
Cresta Gold Rip
Georgia Boy
Golden Beauty of Roedare
Goldenrods Thanksgiving

Harbor City Rebel
Joaquin Nugget
King Midas of Woodend
Kingsdales Buck
Kings Red Flame
Lorelei's Golden Rockbottom
Macopin Expectation
Macopin Maximum
Nickolas of Logan's End
Oakcreek's Freemont
Oakcreek's Sir Doechester
Oakcreek's Van Cleeve — was sterile
Patricia of Roedare

Pirate of Golden Valley
Pride of Roaring Canyon
Ready Always of Marion Hill
Red Ruff
Rip
Rockhaven Raynard of Fo-Ga-Ta
Rock of Roaring Canyon
Rocky Mack
Royal Peter Golden Boy
Royal's Royal of Stonegate
Sheltercove Beauty
Squawkie Mill Dapper Dexter

Stilrovin Katherine
Stilrovin Luke Adew
Stilrovin Nitro Express
Stilrovin Rip's Pride
Stilrovin Super Speed
Stilrovin Tuppee Tee
Sunshine Cake
Tenkahoff Esther Belle
The Golden Kidd
Tristrada Upset
Whitebridge Wally
Zip

Charley Morgan - v. intelligent

CHESAPEAKE BAY RETRIEVERS

Aleutian Mike
Atom Bob
Bayberry Pete
Chesacroft Baron
Chesnoma's Louis
Chuck's Rip Joy
Deerwood Trigger
Dilwyne Montauk Pilot
Guess of Shagwong
Gypsy
Meg's Pattie O'Rouke
Montgomery's Sal

Mount Joy's Mallard
Nelgard's Baron
Nelgard's King Tut
Odessa Creek Sunky
Raindrop of Deerwood
Rip
Shagawong Gypsy
Skipper Bob
Sodak's Gypsy Prince
Sodak's Rip
Star King Mt. Joy
Tiger of Clipper City

AKC Rules Governing Retriever Field Trials

EXCERPTS

Retriever field trials are not run in a haphazard manner; rather, they are governed by a set of rules and recommendations which have been formulated in an effort to achieve greater uniformity in the judging of competing dogs and in the conditions under which said dogs compete. The following excerpts from The American Kennel Club's rules and the *Standing Recommendations of the Retriever Advisory Committee* should not be considered complete or all inclusive: they are reprinted here with the kind permission of The American Kennel Club from whom detailed information may be obtained.

CHAPTER 3

FIELD TRIALS DEFINED AND CLASSIFIED

A MEMBER FIELD TRIAL is a field trial at which championship points may be awarded, given by a club or association which is a member of The American Kennel Club.

A LICENSED FIELD TRIAL is a field trial at which championship points may be awarded, given by a club or association which is not a member of The American Kennel Club, but which has been specially licensed by The American Kennel Club to give the specific field trial designated in the license.

A SANCTIONED FIELD TRIAL is an informal field trial at which dogs may compete but not for championship points, held by a club or association, whether or not a member of The American Kennel Club, by obtaining the sanction of The American Kennel Club.

CHAPTER 5

RIBBONS, MONEY PRIZES, AND SPECIAL PRIZES WHICH MAY BE OFFERED

SECTION 1. All clubs or associations holding field trials under the rules of The American Kennel Club, except sanctioned field trials, shall use the following colors for their prize ribbons or rosettes:

First prize—Blue.
Second prize—Red.
Third prize—Yellow.
Fourth prize—White.
Special prize—Dark Green.

SECTION 2. Each ribbon or rosette, except those used at sanctioned field trials, shall be at least 2 inches wide, and approximately 8 inches long; and bear on its face a facsimile of the seal of The American Kennel Club, the name of the prize, and the name of the field trial-giving club with numerals of year and date of trial.

SECTION 3. If ribbons are given at sanctioned field trials, they shall be of the following colors, but may be of any design or size:

First prize—Rose.
Second prize—Brown.
Third prize—Light Green.
Fourth prize—Gray.

Special prize—A combination of any of these colors.

SECTION 4. If money prizes are offered, a fixed amount for each prize shall be stated.

SECTION 5. All special prizes not money which may be offered shall be accurately described or the value stated. Stud services shall not be accepted as special prizes.

CHAPTER 9

ENTRIES AND ENTRY FEES

SECTION 1. Every dog entered in a licensed or member trial held under the rules of The American Kennel Club must be at least six months of age on the first day of the trial and registered in The American Kennel Club Stud Book or be part of a previously registered litter, excepting pure bred dogs which have won points or credits toward a championship on or before March 13, 1962.

A dog that is part of a registered litter may be entered and run in three trials before it is registered, but only provided the same name is used for the dog each time. No unregistered dog may be entered more than three times unless the owner has received from The American Kennel Club a Listing Notice authorizing further entries for a specified period. The owner may apply by letter to The American Kennel Club for such a listing privilege, explaining the reasons for the delay in registration and demonstrating that it is due to circumstances for which he is not responsible.

All listing notices issued will be void upon the registration of the dog or at the expiration of the period for which the listing has been granted, but upon written application extensions of the listing privilege may be issued.

SECTION 2. Every dog must be entered in the name of the person who actually owned the dog at the time entries closed. The right to enter and run a dog cannot be transferred. A registered dog which has been acquired by some person other than the owner as recorded with The American Kennel Club must be entered in the name of its new owner at any field trial for which entries close after the date on which the dog was acquired, and application for transfer of ownership must be sent to The American Kennel Club by the new owner within seven days after the last day of the trial. The new owner should state on the entry form that transfer application has been mailed to The American Kennel Club or will be mailed shortly. If there is any unavoidable delay in obtaining the completed application required to record the transfer, The American Kennel Club may grant a reasonable extension of time provided the new owner notifies the field trial records department of The American Kennel Club by mail within

seven days after the trial, of the reason for the delay. If an entry is made by a duly authorized agent of the owner, the name of the actual owner must be shown on the entry form. If a dog is owned by an association, the name of the association and a list of its officers must be shown on the entry form.

SECTION 3. The entry must clearly state the name and sex of the dog. The American Kennel Club registration number, the date of birth, name of sire and dam, the name of the breeder, and the name and address of the owner. Should any of these particulars be unknown, it shall be so stated on the entry form.

SECTION 4. No entry shall be received from any person who is not in good standing with The American Kennel Club on the day of the closing of the entries. Before accepting any entries, a list of persons not in good standing must be obtained by the Field Trial Superintendent or Field Trial Secretary from The American Kennel Club.

SECTION 5. No entry shall be made under a kennel name unless that name has been registered with The American Kennel Club. All entries made under a kennel name must be signed with the kennel name followed by the word "registered." An "entrant" is the individual, or, if a partnership, all the members of the partnership entering in a field trial. In the case of such entry by a partnership every member of the partnership shall be in good standing with The American Kennel Club before the entry will be accepted; and in case of any infraction of these rules, all the partners shall be held equally responsible.

SECTION 6. Owners are responsible for errors in making out entry forms, whoever may make such errors.

SECTION 7. No dog which

1. has distemper or other communicable disease shall be entered or run at any field trial.
2. has had distemper or other communicable disease shall be entered or run at any field trial unless it has been fully recovered for thirty days.
3. is known to have been in contact with distemper or other communicable disease shall be entered or run in any field trial until thirty days after such contact and provided said dog has itself been free from any symptom of said disease during said thirty days.
4. has been kenneled on premises on which there existed distemper or other communicable disease shall be entered or run in any field trial until thirty days after such exposure and provided said dog has itself been free from any symptom of said disease during said thirty days.
5. has been inoculated with distemper virus shall be entered or run at any field trial unless

it has been fully recovered from any reaction to said inoculation for at least thirty days.
6. has been inoculated with distemper virus and has shown no reaction thereto shall be entered or run in any field trial until thirty days after said inoculation.
7. is known to have been in contact with an animal which has been inoculated within thirty days with distemper virus shall be entered or run in any field trial until thirty days after such contact, and provided said dog has itself been free from any symptom of distemper during said thirty days.

SECTION 8. A dog is not eligible to be entered in any field trial in any stake in which championship points are given, if the Judge of that stake or any member of his family has owned, sold, held under lease, boarded, trained or handled the dog within one year prior to the date of the field trial.

SECTION 9. Any field trial-giving club which accepts an entry fee other than that published in its premium list or entry form, or in any way discriminates between entrants shall be disciplined. No club or member of any club shall give or offer to give any owner or handler any special inducements, such as reduced entry fees, allowances for board or transportation or other incentive of value for a certain number of entries or shall give or offer to give in consideration of entering a certain number of dogs, any prizes or prize money, except the officially advertised prizes or prize money, which prize money shall be for a stated sum or a portion of the entry fees. Any club found guilty of violating this rule shall be barred from holding licensed or sanctioned trials, and if a member of The American Kennel Club, may be expelled from membership therein. All persons found guilty of paying or receiving any monies, special inducements or allowances in violation of the foregoing shall be disciplined, even to the extent of being deprived of all privileges of The American Kennel Club for a stated time or indefinitely.

SECTION 10. A Field Trial Committee may decline any entries or may remove any dog from its trial for cause, but in each such instance shall file good and sufficient reasons for so doing with The American Kennel Club.

SECTION 11. Any dog entered and present at a field trial must compete in all stakes in which it is entered, unless excused by the Field Trial Committee at that trial after consultation with the Judges.

CHAPTER 15

SPECIAL RULES AND CHAMPIONSHIP POINTS APPLYING TO RETRIEVERS AND IRISH WATER SPANIELS

SECTION 1. Wherever used in this Chapter 15 and in the Standard Procedure for Non-Slip Retriever Trials, the word Retriever shall be deemed to include the several breeds of Retrievers and/or Irish Water Spaniels.

Field trial clubs or specialty clubs formed for the improvement of any one of the several breeds of Retrievers may give field trial stakes in which one of said breeds only may compete, or in which more than one of said breeds may compete together.

Championship points may be awarded where two or more of said breeds compete together in a mixed stake as well as where a separate stake has been provided for each breed.

SECTION 2. ENTRIES. Only pure bred Retrievers over six months of age may be entered in field trials.

The owner or agent entering a dog in a trial does so at his own risk, and agrees to abide by the rules of The American Kennel Club.

A dog is not eligible to be entered in any field trial in any stake in which championship points are given if the judge of that stake or any member of his family has owned, sold, held under lease, boarded, trained or handled the dog within one year prior to the starting date of the field trial.

No post entries will be accepted and entries shall close not later than the time of the drawing which drawing shall take place at least days before the first day of al.

Judges shall have the power to disqualify any dog which shall not appear within fifteen minutes of the time designated for its turn to be tried.

Judges shall have the power to exclude from competition bitches in season or any dog which the judge may consider unfit to compete. The entry fee of all such dogs shall be forfeited except in cases of bitches in season.

SECTION 3. In stakes for Retrievers the order of running shall be decided by lot at the draw, dogs worked by the same person or belonging to the same owner being separated when possible. At the option of the trial-giving club, the drawing may be arranged so that all bitches are drawn after all dogs.

SECTION 4. Only stakes which are run on game birds and on both land and water shall be permitted to carry championship points. Premium lists should specify the kind of game to be used in each stake, and, unless otherwise specified in the premium list, only pheasants and ducks may be used in stakes carrying championship points, and pheasants or pigeons or ducks in other stakes.

SECTION 5. After a Field Trial Committee has selected field trial grounds, no competing dog shall be trained on that part of the grounds to be used for the trials.

SECTION 6. In the event of the weather proving unsuitable for holding the trials, the Field Trial Committee may suspend or postpone any or all stakes up to three days. Notice of such postponement shall be forwarded immediately to The American Kennel Club.

Postponement beyond three days must have the approval of The American Kennel Club.

In the event of postponement of 24 hours or more in the starting time of any stake, any competitor shall have the right to withdraw his entries and his entry fees shall be returned to him.

SECTION 7. The decisions of the Field Trial Committee present shall be final and conclusive in all matters arising at the meeting, and shall bind all parties, subject, however, to the rules of The American Kennel Club.

SECTION 8. Splitting of prizes and/or places at a Retriever Trial is prohibited.

SECTION 9. The regular official stakes at a Retriever Trial shall be Derby, Qualifying, Open All-Age, Limited All-Age, Special All-Age and Amateur All-Age.

A Derby Stake at a Retriever Trial shall be for dogs which are not over two years of age on the first day of the trial at which they are being run. For example, a dog whelped May 1, 1955, would not be eligible for Derby Stakes at a trial starting May 1, 1957, but would be eligible at a trial the first day of which was April 30, 1957.

A Qualifying Stake at a Retriever Trial shall be for dogs which have never won first, second, third, or fourth place or a Judges' Award of Merit in an Open All-Age, Limited All-Age or Special All-Age Stake, or won first, second, third or fourth place in an Amateur All-Age Stake, or won two first places in Qualifying Stakes at licensed or member club trials. In determining whether a dog is eligible for the Qualifying Stake, no award received on or after the date of closing of entries shall be counted.

An Open All-Age Stake at a Retriever Trial shall be for all dogs.

A Limited All-Age Stake at a Retriever Trial shall be for dogs that have previously been placed or awarded a Judges' Award of Merit in an Open All-Age Stake, or that have been placed first or second in a Qualifying or placed or awarded a Judges' Award of Merit in an Amateur All-Age Stake carrying championship points.

A Special All-Age Stake at a Retriever Trial shall be for dogs that have previously during the calendar year in which the Stake is being held or the preceding calendar year been placed or awarded a Judges' Award of Merit in an Open All-Age, Limited All-Age or Special All-Age Stake, or placed or awarded a Judges' Award of Merit in an Amateur All-Age Stake carrying championship points or placed first or second in a Qualifying Stake.

An Amateur All-Age Stake at a Retriever Trial shall be for any dogs, if handled in that stake by persons who are Amateurs (as determined by the Field Trial Committee of the trial-giving club).

SECTION 10. At any field trial, there shall not be more than one of the following stakes:—Open All-Age, Limited All-Age, Special All-Age, and no club shall hold more than two of any of these stakes in one calendar year.

In a two-day trial, when one of the above stakes is held, not more than two other stakes shall be held unless more than one stake is run at the same time under different Judges.

SECTION 11. A National Championship Stake at a Retriever Trial shall be for dogs which by reason of wins previously made qualify under special rules subject to approval by the Board of Directors of The American Kennel Club. This stake shall be run not more than once in any calendar year by a club, or association, formed for this purpose and duly licensed by The American Kennel Club. The winner of such stake shall become a Field Trial Champion of Record if registered in The American Kennel Club Stud Book and shall be entitled to be designated "National Retriever Field Trial Champion of 19—."

SECTION 12. A National Amateur Championship Stake at a Retriever Trial shall be for dogs which by reason of wins previously made, qualify under special rules subject to approval by the Board of Directors of The American Kennel Club. This stake shall be run not more than once in any calendar year by a club or association formed for this purpose, or by the club formed to conduct the National Championship Stake, and the stake shall be duly licensed by The American Kennel Club. The Winner of such stake shall become an Amateur Field Trial Champion of Record if registered in The American Kennel Club Stud Book, and shall be entitled to be designated "National Amateur Retriever Field Trial Champion of 19—."

SECTION 13. Non-regular stakes may be held at Retriever Trials subject to the approval of The American Kennel Club, and provided the premium list sets forth any special conditions regarding eligibility for entry, and any special conditions regarding the method of conducting or judging the stake. Such stakes will not carry championship points or be considered as qualifying a dog for any other stake.

SECTION 14. A Retriever shall become a Field Trial Champion of Record, if registered in The American Kennel Club Stud Book, after having won points in Open All-Age, Limited All-Age or Special All-Age Stakes at field trials of member clubs of The American Kennel Club or at field trials of

non-member clubs licensed by The American Kennel Club to hold field trials.

SECTION 15. A Retriever shall become an Amateur Field Trial Champion of Record, if registered in The American Kennel Club Stud Book, after having won points in Open All-Age, Limited All-Age or Special All-Age Stakes when handled by an Amateur (as determined by the Field Trial Committee of the trial giving club) and in Amateur All-Age Stakes at field trials of member clubs of The American Kennel Club or at trials of non-member clubs licensed by The American Kennel Club to hold trials.

SECTION 16. The total number of points required for a championship, the number of places in a stake for which points may be required, the number of points to be acquired for each place, and the number of starters required and their qualifications for eligibility to acquire points in each stake shall be fixed and determined by the Board of Directors of The American Kennel Club.

At each trial having an Open All-Age Stake, or an Amateur All-Age Stake, the Secretary of the Club in his report must certify whether at least twelve (12) of the starters in each of those stakes were eligible to compete in a Limited All-Age Stake.

At each trial having an Open All-Age, Limited All-Age or Special All-Age Stake, the secretary in his report must specify which handlers of placing dogs, if any, in any of those stakes are determined to be Amateurs by their Field Trial Committee.

At present, to acquire an Amateur Field Championship, a Retriever must win

(1) a National Amateur Championship Stake or (2) a total of 15 points, which may be acquired as follows:— In each Open All-Age, Limited All-Age, Special All-Age, or Amateur All-Age Stake, there must be at least 12 starters, each of which is eligible for entry in a Limited All-Age Stake, and the handler must be an Amateur (as determined by the Field Trial Committee of the trial-giving club), and the winner of first place shall be credited with 5 points, second place 3 points, third place 1 point, and fourth place ½ point, but before acquiring a championship, a dog must win a first place and acquire 5 points in at least one Open All-Age, Limited All-Age, Special All-Age or Amateur All-Age Stake open to all breeds of Retrievers, and not more than 5 points of the required 15 shall be acquired in trials not open to all breeds of Retrievers.

At present, to acquire a Field Championship, a Retriever must win

(1) a National Championship Stake or (2) a total of 10 points, which may be acquired as follows: — In each Open All-Age, Limited All-Age or Special All-Age Stake there must be at least 12 starters, *each of which is eligible for entry in a Limited All-Age Stake, and the winner of first place shall be credited with 5 points, second 3 points, third place 1 point, and fourth place ½ point, but, before acquiring a championship, a dog must win first place and acquire 5 points in at least one Open All-Age, Limited All-Age, or Special All-Age Stake open to all breeds of Retrievers, and not more than 5 points of the required 10 shall be required in trials not open to all breeds of Retrievers.*

STANDARD PROCEDURE FOR NON-SLIP RETRIEVER TRIALS

In order that trials may be conducted as uniformly as practicable, standardization of objectives is essential and, therefore, all Judges, guns, contestants and officials who have a part in conducting trials should be familiar with and be governed so far as possible by the following standard:—

BASIC PRINCIPLES

1. The purpose of a Non-Slip Retriever trial is to determine the relative merits of retrievers in the field. Retriever field trials should, therefore, simulate as nearly as possible the conditions met in an ordinary day's shoot.

Dogs are expected to retrieve any type of game bird under all conditions, and the Judges and the Field Trial Committee have complete control over the mechanics and requirements of each trial. This latitude is permitted in order to allow for the difference in conditions which may arise in trials given in widely separated parts of the United States which difference well may necessitate different methods of conducting tests.

2.   The function of a Non-Slip Retriever is to seek and retrieve "fallen" game when ordered to do so. He should sit quietly in line or in the blind, walk at heel, or assume any station designated by his handler until sent to retrieve. When ordered, a dog should retrieve quickly and briskly without unduly disturbing too much ground, and should deliver tenderly to hand. He should then await further orders.

Accurate marking is of primary importance. A dog which marks the fall of a bird, uses the wind, follows a strong cripple, and will take direction from his handler is of great value.

TRIAL PROCEDURE

3.   The Judges, with due regard to the recommendations of the Field Trial Committee, shall determine the tests to be given in each series—and shall try to give all dogs approximately similar tests in the same series.

4.   At the end of the first series, and every series thereafter, the Judges will call back all dogs which they wish to try further, and will cause them to be run in addi-

tional series until the stake is decided.

5.   Judges shall in their discretion determine the number of dogs that shall be worked or kept on line simultaneously. In at least one series in all stakes, except Derby, every dog should be kept on line off leash while another dog works.

6.   When coming to line to be tested, the dog and its handler should assume any positions directed by the Judges.

In stakes carrying championship points, dogs should be brought to the line and taken from the line off leash and without collar, and remain without collar while under judgment. Dogs should be considered under judgment from the time they are called to come to the line until they have left the line and are back of all the Judges, at which point the dogs may be put on leash.

No dog should run with bandages or tape of any kind without the approval of the field trial committee. The committee should inspect the injury for which bandage or tape is being used unless, of their own knowledge, they already possess such information or unless they are furnished with a veterinary's certificate setting forth this information to their satisfaction.

In other stakes dogs should be taken off leash when they get to the line and remain off leash while they are under judgment.

7.   The dogs should be shot over by guns appointed by the Field Trial Committee, or, at the

option of the Judges, by the handler. In the event of the handler shooting, he should be backed up by official guns.

8. After birds have been shot, all guns shall remain quietly and only move their positions in accordance with specific instructions by Judges.

9. When possible, in land series game should be dropped on fresh territory for each dog and not on ground already fouled.

10. When on line, a handler should not place his dog or himself so that the dog's full vision of any birds or falls is blocked.

11. Unless otherwise instructed by the Judges, no dog should be sent to retrieve until his number has been called by one of the Judges.

12. Judges should call the number of the dog ordered to retrieve rather than the name of the handler or dog.

13. If, when a dog is ordered by the Judge to retrieve a fall, and another dog breaks for the same fall and interferes with the working dog to the extent of causing him in any way to make a faulty performance, the dog interfered with should be considered as not having been tried and given a chance for another performance.

14. When ordered to retrieve, the handler shall direct his dog from any position designated by the Judges.

15. Retrievers should perform equally well on the land and in the water, and should be thoroughly tested on both.

16. During at least one water test in all stakes, dogs should be worked over artificial decoys, anchored separately.

17. In stakes carrying championship points all competing dogs should be kept where they can neither see the falls for another dog nor see any particular dog work in any water series they have not completed.

18. Nothing should be thrown to encourage a dog to enter the water or direct a dog to the fall.

19. In stakes carrying championship points, there should be at least one handling test or blind retrieve—and preferably two, one on land and one in water.

20. All competing dogs must be kept where they cannot see blind retrieves planted and where they cannot see another dog working on a blind retrieve in any series which they have not completed. Members of the Field Trial Committee should report violations of this section to the Judges. Violations of this section should be penalized by elimination of the dog and the handler from the stake.

21. Tests or retrieves which are not to be considered by the Judges at the final summing up should not be held.

JUDGING

Because of its concise statement of purpose, Section 2 of this

Standard Procedure is repeated
here:

2. The function of a Non-
Slip Retriever is to seek and retrieve "fallen" game when ordered to do so. He should sit
quietly in line or in the blind,
walk at heel, or assume any station designated by his handler
until sent to retrieve. When ordered, a dog should retrieve
quickly and briskly without unduly disturbing too much
ground, and should deliver tenderly to hand. He should then
await further orders.

Accurate marking is of primary importance. A dog which
marks the fall of a bird, uses the
wind, follows a strong cripple,
and will take direction from his
handler is of great value.

22. The Judges must judge the
dogs for (a) their natural abilities,
including their memory, intelligence, attention, nose, courage,
perseverance and style, and (b)
their abilities acquired through
training, including steadiness, control, response to direction and delivery.

LINE MANNERS

23. When called to be tested,
a dog should come tractably at
heel and sit promptly at the point
designated by his handler.

No handler shall carry exposed
any training equipment (except
whistle) or use any other equipment or threatening gestures in

such manner that they may be an
aid or threat in steadying or con-
trolling a dog.

24. The dog should remain
quietly where placed until given
further orders.

Retrievers which bark or whine
on line, in a blind or while retrieving should be penalized.

Any dog whose handler is found
holding him to keep him steady
may be eliminated.

Dogs which are restrained on
line noisily or continuously shall
be penalized.

25. In an All-Age Stake, if a
dog makes a movement which in
the opinion of the Judges, indicates
a deliberate intent to retrieve without having been ordered to do so,
that dog shall be deemed to have
broken and shall be eliminated.
In any stake other than an All-
Age Stake, if a dog makes a slight
break and is brought immediately
under control, the dog need not be
penalized for unsteadiness. In all
stakes, after the Judges have directed that a dog be ordered to
retrieve, that dog is entitled to run
in and retrieve and shall not be
accused of or penalized for breaking, even though the Judges did
not see or hear the handler send
the dog.

When a dog that is still in a
stake, but not on line under judgment, breaks for a fall for a dog
under judgment, in such a manner
that the dog or his handler interferes, in the opinion of the Judges,
with the normal conduct of the

stake, that dog shall be eliminated from the stake.

When the handler of a dog under judgment is ordered by the Judges for any reason to pick up his dog, he is still under judgment until he has left the line with his dog and put him on leash and all provisions of Paragraph 25 of the Standard Procedure shall apply until that time.

26. After delivering a bird to his handler, a dog should stand or sit close to his handler until given further orders.

THE RETRIEVE

27. When ordered to retrieve, a dog should proceed quickly and eagerly on land or into the water to marked falls or on the line given him by his handler on falls he has not seen. He should not disturb too much ground or area, and should respond quickly and obediently to any further directions his handler might give him.

28. A dog retrieving a decoy should be eliminated.

29. Upon finding the game, he should quickly pick it up and return briskly to his handler.

A dog should not drop his game on the ground, but distinction should be made between deliberately dropping a bird, and readjusting a bad hold or losing his grip because of a struggling bird or running over uneven terrain.

30. Upon returning, he should deliver the bird promptly and tenderly to his handler. A dog sitting to deliver should not outscore a a dog making a clear delivery without sitting to do so.

31. A dog should be eliminated for hard mouth or badly damaging game, but, before doing so, all Judges should inspect the bird and be satisfied that the dog alone was responsible for the damage.

GENERAL

32. Any handler found kicking, striking or roughly manhandling his dog for any purpose when under judgment may be disqualified for the duration of the stake. Such disqualified handler's dog may continue in the stake under one or more other handlers. For the purpose of this paragraph, a handler is under judgment at any time on or in the vicinity of the field trial grounds during the conduct of the trial when he is seen kicking, striking or roughly manhandling a dog by one or more of the Judges.

33. Judges shall have the power to turn out of the stake any dog which does not obey its handler and any handler who interferes willfully with another handler or his dog.

34. No dog shall be given a place in a stake unless the dog has competed in all tests held for any dog in such stake.

35. The awarding of a Judges' Award of Merit to dogs which have passed every required test in a stake and have shown them-

selves to be well trained and qualified retrievers should be encouraged.

GENERAL PROVISIONS

36. All field trial-giving clubs should clearly recognize that Open, Limited or Special All-Age Stakes are of the first importance and that all other stakes are of relatively lesser importance and are requested to adjust the timing of stakes so that time shall be available for a fair test in these stakes.

37. It is essential that all spectators attending a trial should be kept far enough from the line to enable the dog working to clearly discern his handler and nothing shall be done to distract the dog's attention from his work. A handler has the right to appeal to the Judges if the gallery is interfering with his work in any way and the Judges in their discretion may, if they believe the dog has been interfered with, give him another test.

38. There should be no practicing or training on any part of the field trial grounds from the start of the trial until its conclusion.

39. In sanctioned trials or non-regular stakes, any sections of this Standard Procedure may be relaxed or eliminated, but all contestants should be advised in what respects this is true.

RETRIEVER ADVISORY COMMITTEE RECOMMENDATIONS

The Retriever Advisory Committee has adopted several standing recommendations to all retriever trial-giving clubs, which includes a Supplement to the Standard Procedure, that deals in more detail with the conduct and judging of these trials.

All Officials of trial-giving clubs and Judges should be posted on these recommendations, copies of which are available, upon request, at The American Kennel Club.

The following recommendations of the Retriever Advisory Committee are not rules, but rather what their name implies: recommendations formulated in an effort to achieve greater uniformity in both the conduct and the judging of retriever trials.

Standing Recommendations of the Retriever Advisory Committee

The Retriever Advisory Committee has made the following standing recommendations to all trial-giving clubs (In connection with the first three, the Committee has requested The American Kennel Club, whenever possible, to call the attention of any club, whose application is in violation of any of them, to these recommendations, and to report to the next meeting of the Committee any club that wilfully proceeded in violation after being advised.):

1. Only Amateurs should be asked to judge retriever trials.
2. No cash or merchandise should be given as prizes for placing dogs. There should be no prizes or trophies of any kind offered to handlers in any stake, except (a) trophies to Amateur handlers and (b) a trophy to the handler of the winning dog in the National Championship Stake.
3. In Open, Limited or Special All-Age Stakes, held after July 1, 1959, there should be only two Judges and their combined experience should be such that they have judged a total of five (5) Open, Limited or Special All-Age Stakes.
    In Amateur All-age Stakes, held after July 1, 1959, there should be only two Judges and their combined experience should be such that they have judged a total of five (5) Open, Limit-

ed or Special All-Age Stakes, or Amateur All-Age Stakes since January 1, 1958.
4. Programs should show all the information about competing dogs that is called for in entry blanks.
5. Humane handling and care of game at a trial should be rigidly practiced.
6. The following definition should be used in determining the status of any person to be an Amateur:
    A person shall be considered an Amateur if, in the opinion of the Field Trial Committee of the particular trial, he has not attempted to derive any part of his livelihood from the training, handling or showing of field or hunting dogs in the calendar year of the trial or the preceding calendar year.
7. That a minimum of three and one-half live birds per dog be made available for use in land series in the Open All-Age and Amateur Stakes in any trial carrying championship points and that a minimum of two live birds per dog be made available for use in land series in the Derby and Qualifying Stakes.

8. That the following "Supplement to the Standard Procedure" be used in the conducting and judging of Retriever trials.

INTRODUCTION

The purpose of this supplement is to clarify The American Kennel Club's "STANDARD PROCEDURE FOR NON-SLIP RETRIEVER TRIALS" for all who are in any way concerned with the conduct of a field trial. Consequently, nothing contained herein shall be considered as altering anything in that "STANDARD," but only as advisory in the interpretation of it.

The *objectives* of this supplement are twofold: *First,* greater uniformity in the conduct of retriever trials; and *second,* greater uniformity in the judging of performances by retrievers at those field trials.

The "STANDARD" has been formulated in such a manner that the Officials of a trial-giving club and the Judges have considerable latitude in the conduct of a trial. This is desirable to allow for variations in conditions that are peculiar to various parts of the country, and also to grant Judges unlimited opportunities for ingenuity in planning tests. This supplement is not intented to be restrictive, either to Officials or Judges, as it presents these interpretations of the "STANDARD."

This supplement has been divided into two sections: (1) Trial Procedure and (2) Evaluation of Dog Work. In respect to *trial procedure,* the supplement presents guidance to Judges, Guns and Officials of the trial-giving club in the conduct of the trial, so that it will be well planned and smooth-running, in order that all dogs will be given adequate and relatively equal opportunity to display their merits. In respect to *evaluation of dog work,* the supplement presents guidance to Judges in grading the performances of the dogs so that there will be greater uniformity in the penalties assessed for various faults.

The introductory paragraph of the "STANDARD" states:

"In order that trials may be conducted as uniformly as practiable, standardization of objectives is essential and, therefore, all Judges, Guns, Contestants and Officials who have a part in conducting trials should be familiar with and be governed so far as possible by the following standard. . . ."

It is essential that all concerned with the conduct of retriever field trials, i.e., Field Trial Committee, Marshal, Guns and Judges, as well as the Contestants, shall have read and shall be conversant with the current editions of The American Kennel Club's "Rules Applying to Registration and Field Trials" and its "Standard," as well as this supplement. Such, alone, would do much in attaining that much-desired greater uniformity in both "Trial Procedure" and "Evaluation of Dog Work."

Section 1, a Basic Principle of the "STANDARD" states:

"The purpose of a Non-Slip Retrievers trial is to determine the relative merits of retrievers in the field. Retriever field trials should, therefore, simulate as nearly as possible the conditions met in an ordinary day's shoot.

"Dogs are expected to retrieve any type of game bird under all conditions, and the Judges and the Field Trial Committee have complete control over the mechanics and requirements of each trial. This latitude is permitted in order to allow for the difference in conditions which may arise in trials given in widely separated parts of the United States which difference well may necessitate different methods of conducting tests."

The final phrase in the first paragraph above: *"the conditions met in an ordinary day's shoot,"* should be interpreted for application to field trials, as *"natural hunting conditions."*

Section 2, the other Basic Principle of the "STANDARD," states:

"The function of a Non-Slip Retriever is to seek and retrieve 'fallen' game when ordered to do so. He should sit quietly in line or in the blind, walk at heel, or assume any station designated by his handler until sent to retrieve. When ordered, a dog should retrieve quickly and briskly without unduly disturbing too much ground, and should deliver tenderly to

hand. He should then await further orders.

"Accurate marking is of primary importance. A dog which marks the fall of a bird, uses the wind, follows a strong cripple, and will take direction from his handler is of great value."

While "natural hunting conditions" are subject to great variations in different parts of the U.S.A., the work expected of the dogs should *not* be subject to similar wide variations. In most instances, there should be little doubt in anyone's mind as to the type of work which constitutes a perfect performance in a given test. However, there is unlimited opportunity for an honest difference of opinion on the severity of the penalty to assess for any given infraction or deviation from perfect work.

Therefore, there must always be the possibility of owners and handlers being confused and dismayed because their dog is "dropped" from further competition, or not being included in the placings due to faults which other Judges at other trials had not so severely penalized. However, this should be minimized, for everyone has the right to know which particular faults will be penalized severely, moderately, or only to a minor degree. So, some clarification on these points is needed; hence, there has been included at the conclusion of this supplement a suggested *classification of these various infractions;* they have been divided into three categories, namely: *"Serious Faults," "Moderate Faults,"* and *"Minor Faults."*

TRIAL PROCEDURE

Apportioning Time to the Various Stakes. This is a first and most important consideration in planning the mechanics of a trial and is the joint responsibility of the Judges and the Field Trial Committee. The premium list scheduled the days of the trial and the hour when the trial will start. Those are fixed, definite factors in planning the mechanics; but a Field Trial Committee could expedite its job considerably, if in the entry form it was recorded that the first stake will start at a specified hour on the first day of the trial and that each succeeding stake will follow at the conclusion of the stake which preceded it, rather than stating the specific hour at which any stake will start, except the first one.

Section 36 of the "STANDARD" states:

"All field trial-giving clubs should clearly recognize that Open, Limited or Special All-Age Stakes are of the first importance, and that all other stakes are of relatively lesser importance and are requested to adjust the timing of stakes so that time shall be available for a fair test in these stakes."

Hence, in the apportionment of time, obviously an Open, Limited or Special All-Age must be

given first consideration, the Amateur All-Age Stake merits next consideration, whereas both a Derby and a Qualifying rate less time, because they are of less importance, although one should not be rated as more important than the other.

The following factors also should be considered in apportioning time: (1) the number of entries in each of the various stakes, (2) the quality and quantity of the facilities available at the field trial grounds, (3) the weather, (4) the proximity of sites for various tests, (5) the ease of moving, and the time involved in moving from one test site to another (here one must not forget about the importance of the size of the gallery), and (6) how the noonday feeding problem is to be handled, i.e., with or without a luncheon break.

Inspection of Field Trial Grounds. It is very important that Judges inspect the field trial grounds with representatives of the Field Trial Committee in advance of the scheduled hour for the trial to start, and seek their counsel regarding any peculiarities of the grounds not readily apparent. At that time the Judges should select and determine the nature of each test and its location, preferably for the entire trial. Also, the trial-giving club must provide an efficient organization to conduct the mechanics of the trial; such will do much to reduce to a minimum the delays in starting stakes and in starting various tests in those stakes—providing, of course, that the Judges have previously planned and have instructed the Field Trial Committee about the location of the next test, and the requirements for game, guns, bird boys, boats, decoys, etc.

Planning Tests. The planning of tests is the responsibility of the Judges; it is also one of their most important responsibilities. With good tests, it is much easier to judge the quality of the performances by various dogs than could be true with tests which are so simple and so easy that most of the dogs turn in almost perfect performances, or with tests which are too difficult and time-consuming, or too "tricky," hence, apparently designed to produce many failures or eliminations.

Of primary importance, tests should approximate "natural hunting conditions." Nevertheless, "falls" which are long and out of gun range for the handler are appropriate and proper; they can be justified on the basis either of birds that fly a considerable distance after having been shot, or of those shot by a hunting companion.

On "marked" retrieves, a dog should be able to see a bird in the air and as it falls, since his memory can be tested only when he has seen the "falls." Many factors contribute to a dog's ability to see and mark the "falls": location of the Guns is important; they should be conspicuous and readily identified by the dog; so, too, are the background against which the bird is visualized in flight and the light conditions, as well as the height to which birds are thrown or to which they fly. Further on falls which might be difficult to mark, the Guns may be requested to shoot twice at every bird, to aid dogs in their marking. Judges may request Guns to disappear from sight after their bird is down, but they should not have them move to another position to deliberately mislead the dogs in their marking. On "marked" retrieves, the order in which birds are to be retrieved should not be specified by the Judges, unless it is to be considered a test of control, i.e., a "handling" test.

On "blind" retrieves, wherever possible, the Judges should plan their tests in such a way that they take advantage of *natural hazards,* such as islands, points of land, sand bars, ditches, hedges, small bushes, adjacent heavy cover, and rolling terrain. Despite such natural distractions, it should be possible, at least in theory, for a dog to "find" a well-planned blind retrieve on the initial line from his handler; that he will do so is highly improbable because of those natural hazards, so he must be handled to the "blind." Nevertheless, the test should be so planned that the dog should be "in sight" continuously. A blind retrieve is a test of control, and a dog which is out of sight for a considerable period cannot be said to be under control. Utilizing natural hazards should obviate the need for Judges issuing special instructions about the manner of completing a blind retrieve, other than to "get the meat" by the shortest, fastest, or most direct route.

Ingenuity on the part of Judges should be encouraged, not only in planning customary tests, but also in devising some which are unusual and quite different from those customarily used at field trials. However, all such unusual tests should conform to "conditions met in an ordinary day's shoot," and they should not require complicated instructions about the desired method of completing the test.

Changing tests, after a series has been started, is bad procedure and should be avoided, if at all possible. One way of avoiding such unsatisfactory tests or of avoiding unforeseen and unpredictable situations which would vitiate an apparently proper and sound test, is the practice of running a "test dog" first, in every series—and before any of the competing dogs is brought to line and tested on it. *Use of a "test dog"* at the start of every series is usual practice by some Judges; a "test dog" is used by many Judges under conditions wherein they may entertain doubts about the exact way in which the test may actually go. Some believe that use of a "test dog" is unnecessary and time-consuming; others contend that, in the long run, use of a "test dog" really saves time;

on occasion, it may save embarrassment for Judges.

Judges' Responsibilities on Line. Before a trial is started, before each stake is started, and before each series is started, the Judges must reach certain decisions among themselves about various details, such as the following:

(1) *Instructions to the handler,* as he comes to line regarding the position he is to take, the nature of the test, and any special instructions about the desired method of completing it. If special instructions are to be given, great care must be exercised so that each handler receives the same instructions. Such can be accomplished by summoning all handlers to the line, before the series is started, and then announcing those special instructions to the group, once and for all. If it is not possible to assemble all handlers for such a single announcement, the special instructions can be written and given to the Marshal, who, in turn, should show them to each handler, before he goes on line. Whatever method the Judges decide to adopt, they should be certain that all handlers receive identical instructions.

(2) *Signaling for birds to be thrown.* It is recommended that each set of guns be signaled separately. This creates more uniform timing between falls and also prevents additional birds being shot if a "fall" is unsatisfactory to the Judges. The signaling Judge should be careful that neither his

signaling nor the shadow of it distracts either dog.

(3) *Calling the dog's number* as a signal for the handler to send his dog is proper, but it is not proper to call the dog's name or the handler's name for this purpose. It makes for greater uniformity, as a rule, if one Judge is responsible for all three of the foregoing duties in each series, with the Judges rotating or taking turns at this duty in different series.

(4) Each Judge should be at liberty to say "No," and independently, if in his opinion any "fall" is such or any situation develops that makes for a relatively unfair test for the dog under judgment. Under such conditions the dog should be "picked up" immediately and tested later on a new set of birds, after waiting behind the line until several other dogs have been tested.

Judges should watch the dog being tested and try to determine whether he apparently saw and marked each "fall." It is proper and right to give him another set of birds if he is unable to see the birds and mark the "falls" through no fault of his own but due to a poor flight of the bird, unusual light conditions, striking changes in the background, or any other occurrence which makes for decidedly different conditions from those under which previously-competing dogs had been tested in that series. On the other hand the dog should not be given a new set of birds when failure to mark was of his own doing—either through lack of attention or because his attention was "frozen" on another set of Guns or a previous "fall."

(5) *Every bird retrieved,* and delivered to the handler, *should be inspected* by one of the Judges, preferably not the one who is calling numbers. Failure to inspect retrieved birds must be catalogued as carelessness and as an undesirable practice. It is unfair to all dogs that are being tested—not alone in respect to the question of "hard mouth," but more particularly since it may furnish the explanation for a slow pick-up or some other oddity in a dog's performance. Any unusual condition of a bird, such as being badly "shot up," etc., should be brought to the attention of the Judges. If the same birds are to be used again, those that are injured should be set aside and not used again.

(6) *If a dog is to be picked up and eliminated* for a faulty performance, instructions to that effect should be given by the Judge who is calling the numbers; however, the decision to eliminate must be the consensus of the Judges.

(7) *Running crippled birds, or "runners,"* are always a problem; they create a lack of uniformity in the "falls." Dogs should be able to follow and "find" a "runner," but until a method has been devised whereby all dogs will be tested equally on "runners," an occasional "runner" can create a gross

inequality in the test. Judges may agree that they will treat a "runner" as a "break of the game" and expect that a dog finds the birds shot for him. Or they may agree that a dog is to be picked up as soon as it is recognized that a bird is a "runner," even though he may have already retrieved the other bird or birds in that particular test, and be tested again on a new set of birds; or they may agree to extend the opportunity to get a new set of birds only to dogs whose work up to the time of reaching the "original fall" of the running bird justifies such consideration.

In any case, the Judges should decide in advance how they will deal with the problem of "runners" should it arise.

(8) The encountering of wild birds, rabbits, or other game by the working dog also presents a problem, and sometimes creates great inequalities. Dogs, particularly in All-Age Stakes, should ignore such distractions or be sufficiently under control to be "handled" to the "fall." Judges should decide in advance how they will deal with such a problem, and, as in the case of runners, they may agree to pick up the dog and retest him at a later time, providing they feel that such a distraction was responsible for a faulty performance.

(9) When for any of the reasons mentioned above or any other conditions that may arise which create decidedly different conditions from other dogs the Judges

wish to pick up a dog and test him again, they should, if possible, allow several dogs to run the test before recalling the dog to be re-run.

If the dog has completed a portion of the test when the unfair situation developed, that dog should be judged on the portion of the test completed in his original try, and on the uncompleted portion in the re-run with the following exceptions:

If in the re-run of the previously completed portion of the test, the dog (1) does not complete that portion in accordance with the Judges' instructions for the test or (2) commits any of the "serious faults," listed at the end hereof, he should be penalized or eliminated for such errors in the same manner as the Judges would deal with him regardless of the re-run.

"Moderate faults" or "minor faults" committed in the re-run, on the previously completed portion, should be ignored and the dog judged on his original work.

(10) When on line, if *working dogs creep forward* or *jump* before being sent—short of breaking—the Judges should agree whether they are to be brought to heel before being sent to retrieve. If so, handlers should be informed of this requirement, in advance, and the manner in which they will be advised on line of its application to them. Also, care should be exercised so that this is enforced in such a manner that it does not be-

come grossly unfair for "honoring" dogs.

Also, in the minor stakes, where "controlled" breaks are permissible, the Judges should reach an agreement about the degree they will consider a "controlled" break in contrast to one which will eliminate the dog from further competition; also, they should be in agreement about the severity of the penalties to assess for various degrees of "controlled" breaks.

(11) *Instructions given to the Marshal and the Guns* should be by agreement of the Judges; of course, these may vary from series to series.

Unless otherwise instructed, the *Guns* should remain quietly and not move their position after their bird is down. Guns should volunteer information to the Judges only: (a) if they suspect that their bird may be a "runner"; (b) if a dog is returning with a bird other than the one that had been shot for him, and (c) if there is a significant change in the cover, which may not be apparent to the Judges.

The *Marshal* should call the dogs to line and announce to the Judges the number of the dog about to be tested. He should call back to line any dog which was picked up and was to be retested at a later time—how long such a dog shall be allowed to wait behind the line before retesting shall be by prearrangement with the Judges, and the handler should be told when he is to run again at the time he is picked up.

He shall also obtain the callbacks for the next series from the Judges, and announce them.

Further, the Marshal is responsible for enforcement of Section 37 of the "STANDARD":

"It is essential that all spectators attending a trial should be kept far enough from the line to enable the dog working to clearly discern his handler. . . ."

(12) *Judges should keep sufficiently detailed notes* on each dog's performance to enable them to recall it completely, or at least its outstanding features. Each fault should be noted, even those that are minor. Although the latter may not require that the dog be penalized at that time, repetitions of that fault or commission of various other faults, in succeeding series, may cause the total of faults to assume serious proportions.

(13) To the extent that time permits, *Judges should be generous in their "call backs"* for additional series. No dog should be eliminated from further competition unless it is the consensus of the Judges that it would be impossible for him to "place" in the stake, even though his work in all succeeding series was perfect. For example: Other things being equal, a specific fault, such as failure to mark the "area of the fall," should merit the same penalty in a late series as had been assessed for it in an early series. Actually, the fault committed in the first series may not justify elimination, as

there is no certainty at that time that every other dog may not commit an equally serious fault before the stake is completed. However, commission of that fault in the first series alone may conceivably justify his elimination before the last series is begun, simply because there are several other dogs in competition which, thus far, have not committed any faults and many others whose fault was less serious. Because so little additional testing is contemplated in order to complete the stake, the Judges would be justified in concluding that such an error in the first series, alone, would preclude all probability of that dog being placed in the stake.

(14) Before arriving at their final placings in any stake the *Judges should make direct comparisons, series for series, between all of their dogs under consideration* for those places. Such comparisons permit each Judge to be certain that the dog placed first has given a relatively better performance throughout the stake than the second-place dog, etc. The fourth-place dog should be compared directly with all that are unplaced, and on a similar basis. Judges should be reminded of Section 35 in the "STANDARD" wherein they are encouraged to make a "Judges' Award of Merit" to those dogs which have completed all series, and which show evidence of being well trained and thoroughly qualified retrievers. However, in stakes where a Judges' Award of Merit qualifies a dog for a Limited All-Age Stake and, thus, makes him a starter eligible to make future stakes carry championship points, such awards should not be given unless the dog's work merits this recognition.

Finally, *scoring systems on each series* are of assistance, in general, for preliminary classification of the performances by the various dogs still in competition. They help immeasurably in arriving at a prompt decision after the conclusion of each series, in respect to which dogs should be called back for the next series. However, in the final summation and analysis of the various performances, a direct and detailed comparison of the work by one dog versus the work of another may produce some different conclusions from those suggested by the scores alone. Careful comparisons are heartily recommended, as they are most likely to achieve the true purpose of retriever field trials defined by the "STANDARD" as a method "to determine the relative merits of retrievers in the field."

EVALUATION OF DOG WORK

Judging can never be precise; it is not an exact science, merely an art, simply because there are so many shades of gray between black and white. At the risk of oversimplification, it might be stated that the primary purpose of a retriever is to get the birds to hand as quickly as possible in a pleasing, obedient manner and all faults stem from a deviation from this.

The "STANDARD PROCEDURE FOR NON-SLIP RETRIEVER TRIALS" clearly defines the responsibility of Judges in the first sentence of its "Basic Principles," namely: "to determine the relative merits of retrievers in the field . . ." and, further, while they are performing tests which "simulate as nearly as possible the conditions met in an ordinary day's shoot."

It is recommended that a Judge should have clearly in mind, and for each test, precisely what type of performance he expects, since such work will merit high rating in his records. Then he should observe and record in what respects and to what degrees the performances by individual dogs have either exceeded or fallen short of that previously established "par" in each test. Hence, when the stake is completed, the several Judges will arrive at their final decision about placings on the basis of which dog, relatively, did better work than another in each of the several series.

Therefore, much of a Judge's responsibility is to determine how much weight he shall give to certain types of exceptional performance and how much penalty to assess because of various individual faults, or repetitions of the same fault or combinations of various faults. Some faults in and of themselves are sufficiently serious to *justify elimination* from a stake. Others may justify either a *moder-*

ate penalty, or only a *minor penalty;* and some of the latter may be so minor that on occasion they are relatively so unimportant that for practical purposes they can be ignored. On the other hand, minor faults can summate into moderate or serious faults, and moderate into serious, through repetition or through combinations of several types of faults; such multiplicity of various faults frequently indicates a "failing" or a habitual tendency and results in a performance that is neither a "finished" job nor pleasing to the eye.

Much can be achieved in attaining greater uinformity of judging through a uniformity in definition of the various serious, moderate and minor faults. Tables are included at the end of this section, wherein most of the various faults demonstrated by retrievers are catalogued as: (1) Serious Faults; (2) Moderate Faults; and (3) Minor Faults. However, the personal equation cannot be eliminated completely since each Judge must determine the relative seriousness of individual faults, repetition of faults, or combinations of faults, which occur in the performance by dogs in a particular trial.

Section 22 of the "STANDARD" states:

"The Judges must judge the dogs for (a) their natural abilities, including their memory, intelligence, attention, nose, courage, perseverance and style, and (b) their abilities acquired through training, including steadiness, control, response to direction and delivery."

Natural abilities are of great importance in *all stakes,* whereas *abilities acquired through training* are of less importance in the Qualifying Stake than in those carrying championship points, and are of comparatively minor importance in the Derby Stake.

Natural Abilities

(1) *Accurate marking, or memory of "falls" is of paramount importance.* However, this does not imply that dogs which excel in marking shall not be severely penalized, or even eliminated, for deficiencies in or a lack of the other required "abilities." However, in Derby stakes the ability to "mark" is all-important; even in our most exacting stakes, tests are usually so devised that "marked" birds constitute a large percentage of the retrieves by which each dog's performance is judged.

Ability to "mark" does not necessarily imply "pinpointing the fall." A dog that misses the "fall" on the first cast but recognizes the depth of the "area of the fall," stays in it, then quickly and systematically "hunts it out," has done both a creditable and an intelligent job of marking. Such work should not be appreciably outscored by the dog that "finds" or "pinpoints" on his first cast. However, a dog which consistently, i.e., during an entire stake, marks his birds in a closer area, hence, more accurately than another dog, should be judged accordingly. All things are relative and, conceivably, such differences in marking alone might be sufficient to determine the final placings in a particular stake.

Even with "marked" birds, a handler may be able to render great assistance to his dog by giving him "a line" in the direction of the "fall"; however, there is nothing he can do, short of handling, to aid the dog in recognizing the "depth of the fall." Often a dog gives definite indication of "memory," and of his marking ability, at or after delivery of a first bird, by aligning himself toward or by looking eagerly in the exact direction of an unretrieved "fall"; at times, even leaving at once or leaving on command, but without benefit of a precise line to the "fall" given to him by the handler. There is no invariable method by which the relative merits of such perfect completions can be judged; the dog trained to come to heel and to be lined by the handler briskly and precisely and in the same manner for each and every retrieve, including the first, cannot be penalized for his work—not even relatively, in comparison with a more spontaneous type of performance. However, conspicuously intensive "lining" of dogs to marked falls is undesirable and may be penalized.

What precisely constitutes the *"area of the 'fall,'"* defies accurate definition; yet, at the outset of every test, each Judge must arbitrarily define its hypothetical boundaries for himself and for each bird in that test so that he can judge whether dogs have remained within his own concept of the "area of the 'fall,'" as well as how far they have wandered away from "the area" and how much cover they have disturbed unnecessarily. In determining these arbitrary and hypothetical boundaries of the "area of the 'fall,'" due consideration should be given to various factors: (1) the type, the height and the uniformity of the cover, (2) light conditions, (3) direction of the prevailing wind and its intensity, (4) length of the various falls, (5) the speed of individual dogs, (6) whether there is a change in cover (as from stubble to plowed ground, or to ripe alfalfa, or to machine-picked corn, etc.) or whether the "fall" is beyond a hedge, across a road, or over a ditch, etc., and finally and most important, (7) whether one is establishing the "area of the fall" for a single, or for the first bird a dog goes for, in multiple retrieves, or for the second or the third bird, since each of these should differ from the others.

In general, the "area of the fall" for a single should be relatively small; the area for a first retrieve in a "double" should be smaller than for the second bird, and both of these should be larger in a "triple," and larger still for the third bird in it. Also, "the area" for short retrieves should certainly be smaller than for longer retrieves. Since there are so many conditions and variables to be taken into consideration, it is obvious that each Judge, and for every series, must attempt to define for himself a hypothetical "area of the fall" for each bird, and then judge the dogs accordingly. However, the penalties inflicted should vary in their severity, depending on the distance which individual dogs wander out of the area, the frequency of such wanderings, the number of birds mismarked in a given test, and by the amount of cover disturbed in these meanderings.

Dogs which disturb cover unnecessarily, clearly well out of the area of the "fall," either by not going directly to that area or by leaving it, even though they eventually find the bird without being handled, should be penalized more severely than those handled quickly and obediently to it.

(2) *Intelligence* is a quality not often tested intentionally, since few tests can be designed for that specific purpose. Nevertheless, on occasion, dogs may have an opportunity to demonstrate an unusual degree of intelligence, or lack of it, through the manner in which certain performances are completed. When those occasions arise, and usually they develop by chance rather than by intent, each dog must be credited or penalized on the basis of the intelligence demonstrated.

(3) *Attention* is displayed, even as a dog comes "on line." His eagerness and general attitude

when coming on line, his alertness in locating the "Guns," in acceding to his handler's commands, and in his zeal for the hunt, are highly desirable traits. Conversely, lack of attention and lack of interest should be penalized.

(4) Most retrievers have a *"good nose,"* and, as a rule, they have numerous opportunities to demonstrate this all-important quality at every trial. Usually it is something in his work which suggests that a dog *lacks a good nose* that attracts the Judges' attention. Such suspicion should be recorded so that it can be verified or eliminated by his performance in subsequent tests. On the other hand, scenting conditions are so mysterious and are so little understood, although obviously affected by many factors—such as type of cover, wind, frost, rain, location of "fall," acidity of soil and apparently many other conditions—that extreme caution must be exercised before a dog is charged with a "poor nose" and penalized accordingly.

(5) *Courage,* too, is a trait which cannot be tested at every trial. It may be displayed by a willingness to face, and without hesitation, rough cover, cold or rough water, ice, mud, or other similar conditions which make the going rather tough, *and of doing it repeatedly.* The facilities of trial grounds, or the weather, do not often supply the proper situation for a series specifically designed to test the dogs' courage. Because

the facilities or weather necessary to such a test are often limited, such tests should usually come late in a trial, unless there are reasonable grounds for assumption that all dogs will receive comparable tests. When such tests can be arranged, they are frequently of great value to the Judges in evaluating their relative merits in this highly desirable trait which all retrievers should possess.

(6) *Perseverance* is shown by a dog's determination to stick at it and complete the task at hand, i.e., systematically, aggressively and without faltering, to search for and make the "find" of the bird he has been sent to retrieve. A lack of perseverance may become apparent whenever: (1) he returns to the handler voluntarily and before finding the bird; (2) he either stops his hunt or continues it in a slow, lackadaisical, disinterested manner; (3) the dog "pops up" or looks back to his handler for directions on a "marked fall" and before he has hunted for a considerable time; (4) he "switches birds," and (5) he "blinks" a bird, i.e., fails to pick it up, actually leaves it after making the "find." Most of these are serious faults and should be judged accordingly.

"Switching birds" implies that a dog gives up in his hunt after a a search, leaves "the area," and goes for another bird, or when he drops a bird he is retrieving and goes for another; however, except in the latter case, a dog should not be judged as "switching" unless he goes to the "area" of a "fall," hunts, fails to find, and then leaves that area to hunt for another "fall." Furthermore, it should *not be considered* as a lack of perseverance if while on the way to one "fall" he sees or winds another bird and retrieves it first, or if on the way to one "fall" but long before he reaches "the area" of that "fall" he changes his direction (for some reason or other) and goes for another bird.

(7) *Style* is apparent in every movement of a dog and throughout his entire performance at trials, for example: by the *gaiety* of his manner in approaching the line, by his *alertness* on line, by his *eagerness* and *speed* on retrieves, by his *water entry,* by his *pick-up* of birds, and by his *return* with them. Style makes for a pleasing performance; <u>together with ability to mark, they constitute the most important</u> factors for placings in <u>Derby Stakes</u>.

In all stakes, in respect to "style," a desired performance includes: (a) an alert and obedient attitude, (b) a fast-determined departure, both on land and into the water, (c) an aggressive search for the "fall," (d) a prompt pick-up, and (e) a reasonably fast return. Dogs may be credited for outstanding and brilliant exhibitions of style, or they may be penalized for deficiencies in style— the severity of the penalty ranging from a minor demerit to elimination from the stake, in extreme cases.

(8) Section 31 of the "STANDARD" states:

"A dog should be eliminated for hard mouth or badly damaging game, but, before doing so, all Judges should inspect the the bird and be satisfied that the dog alone was responsible for the damage."

"Hard mouth" is one of the most severely penalized faults in a retriever; furthermore, once a dog has been charged with this fault, he carries that stigma for life. Therefore, "hard mouth" should only become the Judges' verdict when there is incontrovertible proof of it. Torn skin or flesh, alone, is *not* sufficient evidence, in almost all cases, to constitute such proof, since damage of that type may be caused in a variety of ways, such as by sharp sticks and stones, etc., in the cover; also, dogs can unintentionally damage birds when making retrieves from heavy cover, as well as by their fast, "positive" pick-up. Furthermore, at certain times of the year, birds are particularly susceptible to such damage.

Even the fact that a dog delivers a dead bird, when a live one was the object of his retrieve, does not necessarily constitute proof of "hard mouth," as the bird could have died from other causes (particularly true with "shackled" young ducks).

On the other hand, crushed bone structure usually can be accepted as trustworthy and sufficient evidence of "hard mouth."

This is the only evidence offering such proof, in the absence of a particularly obvious, flagrant and unjustified violation of tearing of flesh.

Other faults are frequently confused with "hard mouth," although, in reality, they are entirely separate and distinct from it— even though, in addition, the dog may actually be hard-mouthed. "Freezing," in particular, falls into this category. A hard-mouthed dog may have a gentle delivery and, certainly, a sticky delivery does not imply hard mouth. "Rolling-a-bird" or "mouthing" it, while making the retrieve, may be erroneously associated with "hard mouth" in the opinion of some, even though the bird is not damaged thereby. If such "mouthing" is a fault at all, then it is one of only minor importance.

Judges should remember that a dog is either found to have a "hard mouth" or he is not so found, and, if guilty, he must be eliminated from the stake— other various types of inconclusive evidence should merely be recorded in the Judge's notes, pending the manner in which birds are handled in subsequent series.

While not required, it is a considerate gesture on the part of the Judges to keep separately any bird for which they are eliminating a dog for "hard mouth," and show it to the handler of the dog at a later time, inconspicuously.

Abilities Acquired through Training

The other group of attributes to be considered by Judges includes those abilities which dogs acquire through training. The importance of these acquired qualities varies in different stakes, for example: A "reasonable" degree of steadiness and general obedience are the requirements in Derby stakes. A greater degree of steadiness and some degree of the other qualities are expected in the Qualifying stake. There should be expectation of full refinement in "acquired attributes" in those stakes carrying championship points.

(1) *Steadiness* to the extent of defining what constitutes a "break," is clearly presented in Section 25 of the "STANDARD." However, a degree of amplification might be helpful: Dogs on line sometimes make various types of movements when game is in the air (and/or when it is shot). Such movements may be interpreted as efforts by the dog to improve his view of the "fall," and some occur through sheer excitement. *Some dogs creep forward* from the line, as birds are shot. *If the handler makes no effort* to stop or restrain them, a Judge should not interpret such as a deliberate intent to retrieve, since nothing was done to stop the dog. On the other hand, *if the handler does make an effort* to stop his dog, a Judge should assume that the handler believed the dog intended to retrieve and should deal with such infraction accordingly.

A dog should not be penalized

for a command to sit as the first bird is being thrown on a "walk up." In other tests, a dog should not be penalized for a quiet command to sit as the first bird is being thrown, provided the dog is not in motion and the command is, therefore, not to stop a motion with intent to retrieve.

Except for an occasional change in position in order to better see a "fall," all such movements should be penalized as unsteadiness—the degree of penalty depending on the extent and the frequency of repetition of the offense or offenses. It is proper for Judges, if they so wish, to require that dogs which have jumped or crept forward a predetermined distance (usually a few feet ahead of the handler) be brought back to heel, before being sent for their birds. The requirement of steadiness is a very important factor in judging the work of retrievers.

(2) *Control* is closely allied to the dog's response to direction, but it also includes obedience at all times. Control also includes "line manners," walking tractably "at heel," assuming and staying in any designated position on line, as well as remaining quietly on line beside the handler after delivery of the bird to him. When called, a dog should return promptly to his handler—particularly in those instances where Judges decide that he shall be tested again, at a later time, either because another dog "broke" or due to any one of a variety of other circumstances.

In Derby and Qualifying Stakes, dogs may be brought to the line, and taken from the line, on leash, unless the Judges specify otherwise.

Article 24 of the "STANDARD" provides that dogs shall be penalized if they are noisily or continuously restrained by their handlers while "on line." The degree of the penalty should correspond to the extent and frequency of repetition of the infraction. Although such is not required, it is a considerate gesture by Judges, if they are in agreement, to notify handlers when their methods of restraint are incurring penalties for their dogs.

(3) *Response to direction* is all-important in handling tests—also whenever a dog must be brought back to the "area of the 'fall,'" when he has mismarked. In such response to direction, a dog should take the *original line* given to him by his handler and *continue* on it until he either makes the "find," or until stopped by the handler and given a new line. He should then continue in this new direction until he "finds," or is given further directions, etc.

Faults, or justifications for penalties, include the following: (a) not taking the line originally given by the handler, (b) not continuing on that line for a considerable distance, (c) stopping voluntarily, i.e., "popping up" and looking back for directions, (d) failure to stop promptly and look to the handler, when signaled, (e) failure to take a new direction, i.e., a new cast, when given, and (f) failure to continue in that new direction for a considerable distance.

The seriousness of the penalty for any or all of the foregoing faults varies with the seriousness of the infraction, whether that infraction was repeated and how often, and whether there was a combination of various infractions. However, before inflicting a severe penalty because of a dog's failure to stop promptly at the whistle, Judges should determine whether the wind, the cover, or the distance seriously interfered with the dog's ability to hear his handler. In general, the performance in the test should be considered in its entirety; an occasional failure to take and hold a direction may be considered a minor fault, if offset by several other very good responses. A considerable penalty should be imposed for repeated, willful disobedience of the handler's orders; and less penalty when, after taking the proper direction, he does not continue on it as far as the handler desired. Stopping voluntarily, to look back for directions, in an isolated instance, may be considered a minor fault, but frequent repetition may convert such "popping up" into the category of serious faults.

Delivery of the bird should be made to the handler directly, upon return from the retrieve; it should be given up willingly. A dog should not drop the bird before delivering it; and he should not "freeze," or be unwilling to give

it up. He should not jump after the bird, once the handler has taken it from him. Penalties for faulty delivery may range from minor for an isolated minor offense, to elimination from the stake either for a severe "freeze" or because of repeated moderate infractions.

Classification of Faults

Classification of the many faults which may be exhibited by retrievers during the course of a trial shall be primarily in terms of generalizations. In the lists which follow, various infractions are catalogued as I. SERIOUS FAULTS: II. MODERATE FAULTS: and III. MINOR FAULTS. Each fault should be considered as a single occurrence, and only to an average degree. However, such infraction may be so minor in degree that it scarcely merits the indicated penalty. Conversely the degree of a given instance of infraction may be of sufficient gravity to merit a much more severe penalty than is suggested—even to the point of elimination from the stake. Also, in each of these three general categories, all of the faults listed should not be given equal weight, since they are not of equal gravity or importance.

Repetition of a fault, particularly time after time, indicates a "weakness" or a bad habit, and justifies much more penalty than in an isolated occurrence of this fault. The same holds true when there is a combination of different faults.

The listing of individual faults within each category has not been made in the order of their seriousness but in the order of the foregoing comments about Judging. To these have been added various excerpts from the "STANDARD."

The faults included in this classification are limited to those which are observed most often at retriever trials. Others may occur and this classification may serve as a helpful guide on such occasions in determining the relative importance of such unusual offenses.

Finally, the primary consideration of Judges in respect to the importance of faults here listed, as well as others which may occur, is to determine the extent to which any and all such infractions would detract from the full enjoyment of "an ordinary day's shoot." A Judge may be thoroughly justified in moderating a penalty or even in failing to impose one, if, in his opinion, there have been extenuating circumstances to justify such action.

SERIOUS FAULTS. (In and of themselves, these are usually sufficient to justify elimination from the stake.)

1. Repeated evidence of "poor nose."
2. Reluctance to enter either rough cover, water, ice, mud, or any other situation involving unpleasant or difficult "going" for the dog, after having been ordered to do so several times.

3. Returning to his handler, either without the bird or without having been called in.
4. Stopping his hunt.
5. "Switching birds," i.e., giving up after a search for one bird, and going to "the area" of another "fall," or dropping a bird he is retrieving, and going for another.
6. "Blinking the bird," i.e., ignoring it when found, and leaving it.
7. Restraint by touching or holding a dog, to prevent him from "breaking."
8. "Out of control," i.e., paying no attention to many whistles and directions by the handler.
9. Extreme "freeze," i.e., unwillingness to release a bird on delivery until compelled to do so by severe methods.
10. Retrieving a decoy, i.e., returning to land with it—mandatory elimination under the "STANDARD."
11. *Breaking*—Clear violation of Section 25 of the "STANDARD": mandatory elimination under the "STANDARD."
12. "Hard mouth," or badly damaging game which, in the opinion of the Judges, was caused entirely and solely by the dog without justification—mandatory elimination under the "STANDARD."
13. Loud and prolonged whining or barking.
14. Watching <u>blind</u> retrieves being planted or being retrieved by another dog—

mandatory elimination of both the dog and the handler from the stake under the "STANDARD."

15. Watching birds being shot or retrieved by another dog in a water test, in stakes carrying championship points.

16. Deliberate blocking by a handler so that a dog will not see all birds and all "falls"; this applies both to the "working" dog and the "honoring" dog.

17. Throwing anything into the water to persuade a dog to enter or to direct him to a "fall."

18. Failure to find a dead bird which the dog should have found.

MODERATE FAULTS. (Infractions in this category may actually be so slight as to warrant their consideration as only a "minor" fault, or they may be so severe as to warrant their consideration as a "serious fault"; also, repetitions of a "moderate" fault or a combination of several of these faults may readily convert the total infraction into a "serious" fault.)

1. Failure to mark the "area of the 'fall,'" requiring that the dog he handled to it—worse on a "single," or first bird in a "double," or a "triple" than on either the second or third bird a dog goes for.

2. Leaving "the area" or not going to it, and disturbing too much cover.

3. Reluctance to enter rough cover, water, ice, mud or other situations involving unpleasant "going" for the dog.

4. Hunting in a slow, disinterested, lackadaisical manner, either at once or after a short search.

Poor style, including a disinterested attitude, a slow or reluctant departure, quest for game, or return with it.

6. "Popping up," i.e., looking back for directions on a "marked" bird before an extensive search.

7. Noisily or frequently restraining the dog from breaking, except in extraordinary circumstances.

8. Not stopping for a direction, after two or three whistles which he should have heard.

9. Deliberate failure to take lines and various directions given to him; failure to hold lines and directions more than a short distance.

10. Moderate whining of short duration.

11. Going out of his way by land to a "fall," *without certainty of purpose* to avoid going into the water in a water retrieve.

MINOR FAULTS. (Either severe, or repeated, or combination of these "minor" infractions may summate into a "moderate" or even a "serious" fault. Also, they may be so slight as not to warrant any penalty at all.)

1. Going out of his way by land, without certainty of purpose, on the return from a water retrieve.
2. Lack of attention.
3. Poor line manners; "heeling" poorly; not immediately taking and staying in the position designated; dropping a bird at delivery; jumping after a bird; not remaining quietly on line after delivery.
4. Slow pick-up of a dead bird (except when fluttering or badly shot-up); dropping a bird; handling game in a sloppy manner.
5. "Leg lifting" *particularly* on the way to a "fall."
6. Unsteadiness on line, including creeping.
7. Slight and isolated instances of "hissing" at the dog.
8. Not stopping at the first whistle he should have heard, but stopping at the second or third.
9. Looking back for a direction in a "blind" retrieve, before taking a line or a cast, for a reasonable distance.
10. Occasional failure to take the handler's directions.
11. Occasional failure to hold the line, or directions given, for more than a few yards.
12. Slight "freezing," or reluctance to give up a bird.
13. Slight short whining or one bark, on being sent to retrieve.
14. Roughness with game.

Clubs Holding Field Trials

This list of retriever field trial clubs not only will help you find a field trial if such is your desire, but also will serve as a means of putting you in touch with people who are keenly interested in retrievers and who will gladly assist you with any problem or question you may have. Feel free to write any of the various club secretaries listed.

The three clubs listed below are "breed clubs" and each has nation-wide membership and interest. You may wish to join the one that represents your retriever's breed.

AMERICAN CHESAPEAKE CLUB   c/o
Mr. Charles Sambrailo, Box 404, Watsonville, Calif.

GOLDEN RETRIEVER CLUB OF AMERICA   c/o
Mr. Thomas V. Novak, Rt. 4, Box 256, Mosinee, Wis.

LABRADOR RETRIEVER CLUB   c/o
Mr. C. A. Griscom III, 123 S. Broad St., Philadelphia, Pa.

The following is a list of clubs holding at least one Licensed trial each year. In addition to these Licensed trials, some of the clubs hold Sanctioned or Fun trials during the so-called off season. For your convenience they are listed by states rather than alphabetically.

ALABAMA

MOBILE AMATEUR RETRIEVER CLUB   c/o
Dr. T. H. Bender, 1457 Springhill Ave., Mobile, Ala.

ARIZONA

SOUTHERN ARIZONA RETRIEVER CLUB   c/o
Mr. Edward Shaul, 608 Arizona Land & Title Bldg., Tucson, Ariz.

CALIFORNIA

CALIFORNIA SOUTH COAST RETRIEVER CLUB   c/o
Mr. F. T. Kemp, 210 W. Seventh St., Los Angeles 14, Calif.

LASSEN RETRIEVER CLUB   c/o
Mr. Siebert Stevens, 2249 Canal Dr., Redding, Calif.

NORTHERN CALIFORNIA RETRIEVER TRIAL CLUB   c/o
Mr. Andrieus A. Jones, Hillsborough, Calif.

REDWOOD EMPIRE RETRIEVER CLUB   c/o
Mrs. Ruby G. McGrew, 659 South Redwood Hwy., Fortuna, Calif.

SAGEHEN'S RETRIEVER CLUB   c/o
Mrs. E. J. Rowe, 174 Winchester St., Daly City, Calif.

SOUTHERN CALIFORNIA RETRIEVER CLUB   c/o
Mrs. E. R. Spaulding, 4705 Foothill Rd., Santa Barbara, Calif.

COLORADO

PIKES PEAK RETRIEVER CLUB   c/o
Mrs. Dorothy F. Raber, 927 N. Hancock St., Colorado Springs, Colo.

ROCKY MOUNTAIN RETRIEVER CLUB   c/o
Mr. E. L. Anderson, 7774 Raritan, Denver 21, Colo.

CONNECTICUT

NUTMEG RETRIEVER CLUB   c/o
Mrs. George H. Flinn, Jr., North St., Greenwich, Conn.

DELAWARE

DEL BAY FIELD TRIAL CLUB   c/o
Mr. V. B. Derrickson, Jr., Box 626, Dover, Del.

IDAHO

IDAHO RETRIEVER CLUB   c/o
Mr. R. F. Kloepfer, 117 N. Roosevelt St., Boise, Idaho

SNAKE RIVER RETRIEVER CLUB   c/o
Mr. D. L. Burnett, Pocatello, Idaho

ILLINOIS

AMERICAN AMATEUR RETRIEVER CLUB   c/o
Mr. M. K. Anderson, Box 110, Wasco, Ill.

MIDWEST FIELD TRIAL CLUB   c/o
Dr. George H. Gardner, 720 N. Michigan Ave., Chicago 11, Ill.

IOWA

NORTHWEST IOWA DOG CLUB   c/o
Mr. P. E. Beckwith, 619 Fourth Ave. S.E., Spencer, Iowa

KANSAS

KANSAS CITY RETRIEVER CLUB   c/o
Mr. Robert W. Ryan, 8821 Catalina, Overland Park, Kans.

LOUISIANA

NORTH LOUISIANA RETRIEVER CLUB   c/o
Mr. Thomas Fortenberry, Jr., 1700 Frances Place, Monroe, La.

MAINE

MAINE RETRIEVER TRIAL CLUB   c/o
Mrs. Zelma C. Clark, 547 Ferry Rd., Saco, Maine

MARYLAND

MARYLAND RETRIEVER CLUB   c/o
Mr. E. E. Stickell, 572 Edmondson Ave., Baltimore 28, Md.

TALBOT RETRIEVER CLUB   c/o
Mrs. W.E. Shannahan, RFD 4, Easton, Md.

MASSACHUSETTS

COLONIAL RETRIEVER FIELD TRIAL CLUB   c/o
Mr. Austin B. Mason, Jr., Simon Willard Rd., Concord, Mass.

MICHIGAN

WOLVERINE RETRIEVER CLUB   c/o
Mrs. Susan Cary, Square Lake Rd., Birmingham, Mich.

MINNESOTA

CENTRAL MINNESOTA RETRIEVER CLUB   c/o
Mr. Larry H. Rieder, 111 Fifth Ave., St. Cloud, Minn.

DULUTH RETRIEVER CLUB   c/o
Mr. Roy Peterson, 3804 W. Sixth St., Duluth, Minn.

MINNESOTA FIELD TRIAL ASSOCIATION   c/o
Mr. A. Wells Wilbor, 9200 Wayzata Blvd., Minneapolis 26, Minn.

TRI STATE HUNTING DOG ASSOCIATION   c/o
Mr. Ralph G. Bloat, Watkins Products, Inc., Winona, Minn.

MISSOURI

MISSISSIPPI VALLEY KENNEL CLUB   c/o
Mr. Robert W. Pitts, 10445 Schuessler Rd., St. Louis 28, Mo.

MONTANA

HELENA RETRIEVER CLUB   c/o
Mr. Ray E. Olson, Ennis, Mont.

MONTANA RETRIEVER CLUB   c/o
Mr. Wesley Te Winkle, 2021 Avenue 'H', Billings, Mont.

WESTERN MONTANA RETRIEVER CLUB   c/o
Mrs. Wanda Alsaker, 1308 Jackson, Missoula, Mont.

NEBRASKA

CENTRAL NEBRASKA RETRIEVER CLUB   c/o
Mr. Robert B. Ray, Box 66, Hastings, Nebr.

NEBRASKA DOG AND HUNT CLUB   c/o
Mr. Walter Somerhiser, 2810 N. Cotner, Lincoln, Nebr.

MISSOURI VALLEY HUNT CLUB   c/o
Mr. Frank Holliday, Route 6, Florence Station, Omaha, Nebr.

NEVADA

SIERRA NEVADA RETRIEVER CLUB   c/o
Mrs. M. W. Beck, Box 1137, Carson City, Nev.

NEW JERSEY

SHREWSBURY RIVER RETRIEVER CLUB   c/o
Mrs. Richard Metcalf, RFD 1, Atlantic Highlands, N.J.

NEW YORK

CENTRAL NEW YORK RETRIEVER CLUB   c/o
Dr. James Mithoefer, Cooperstown, N.Y.

LONG ISLAND RETRIEVER TRIAL CLUB   c/o
Mr. August Belmont, Box 22, Syosset, L.I., N.Y.

WESTERN NEW YORK RETRIEVER CLUB   c/o
Mrs. Roland H. Simmons, Robson Rd., Middleport, N.Y.

WOMEN'S FIELD TRIAL CLUB   c/o
Mrs. Milton D. Orowitz, Box 416, Roslyn Heights, L.I., N.Y.

NORTH DAKOTA

NORTH DAKOTA RETRIEVER CLUB   c/o
Dr. V. B. Keltgen, Fourth St., Fargo, N. Dak.

MINOT RETRIEVER CLUB   c/o
Dr. M. D. Hoffman, 203 First National Bank Bldg., Minot, N. Dak.

OHIO

BUCKEYE RETRIEVER CLUB   c/o
Mrs. R. W. Boston, Breezevale Cove, Rocky River 16, Ohio

OHIO VALLEY RETRIEVER CLUB   c/o
Mr. James J. Anderson, 960 Forest Ave., Glendale, Ohio

OREGON

OREGON RETRIEVER TRIAL CLUB   c/o
Mrs. K. L. Carpenter, Route 1, Box 66, Portland 10, Oreg.

ROGUE VALLEY RETRIEVER CLUB   c/o
Mrs. Margaret A. Denman, 104 Geneva, Medford, Oreg.

SHASTA CASCADE RETRIEVER CLUB   c/o
Mrs. Doris L. Kelley, 2019 Manzanita St., Klamath Falls, Oreg.

WILLEMETTE VALLEY RETRIEVER CLUB   c/o
Mrs. Frank S. Walker, 1130 East Front Ave., Albany, Oreg.

PENNSYLVANIA

SWAMP DOG CLUB FOR TRAINING AND TRIALS   c/o
Mrs. C. C. Harrison III, 840 Church Rd., Wayne, Pa.

SOUTH DAKOTA

SIOUX VALLEY RETRIEVER CLUB   c/o
Mrs. D. R. Progulske, 1412 Third St., Brookings, S. Dak.

TENNESSEE

MEMPHIS AMATEUR RETRIEVER CLUB   c/o
Mrs. Ford Graham, Route 2, Nesbitt, Miss.

TEXAS

ALAMO RETRIEVER FIELD TRIAL CLUB   c/o
Mr. L. B. Reppert, 643 Elizabeth Rd., San Antonio, Tex.

LONE STAR RETRIEVER CLUB   c/o
Mr. Milton H. West, 2200 Gulf Bldg., Houston 2, Tex.

NORTH TEXAS RETRIEVER CLUB   c/o
Mrs. Clifford M. Boone, 4254 Summit Ridge Dr., Dallas 16, Tex.

PORT ARTHUR RETRIEVER CLUB   c/o
Mr. J. W. Henderson, Box 3122, Port Arthur, Tex.

UTAH

GREAT SALT LAKE RETRIEVER CLUB   c/o
Miss Barbara Stubblefield, 219 "F" St., Salt Lake City, Utah

WASHINGTON

NORTHWEST RETRIEVER TRIAL CLUB   c/o
Mr. J. J. Heneghan, 3010 First Ave., Seattle, Wash.

PUDGET SOUND RETRIEVER CLUB   c/o
Mr. J. W. Brown, Jr., 36 Harrison Bldg., Bremerton, Wash.

SAMISH RETRIEVER CLUB   c/o
Mr. Harold Loop, 221 First, Mount Vernon, Wash.

SPOKANE RETRIEVER TRIAL CLUB   c/o
Mrs. Lloyd Stokes, 10820 East Valleyway, Spokane, Wash.

TACOMA RETRIEVER CLUB   c/o
Mr. W. C. Ristine, 10014 Norwood Dr. S.W., Tacoma, Wash.

WISCONSIN

MADISON RETRIEVER CLUB   c/o
Mr. W. S. Piper, Frosty Lane, Madison, Wis.

MANITOWAC COUNTY KENNEL CLUB   c/o
Mr. C. E. Allen, 1514 Waldo Blvd., Manitowac, Wis.

SUPERIOR RETRIEVER CLUB   c/o
Mr. Robert L. Hagen, Station B, Route 2, Box 170A, Superior, Wis.

WISCONSIN AMATEUR FIELD TRIAL CLUB   c/o
Mr. John Fraser, 757 N. Broadway, Milwaukee 2, Wis.

WYOMING

BIG HORN BASIN RETRIEVER CLUB   c/o
Mr. H. W. Julien, 1308 Sunset Blvd., Cody, Wyo.

CHEYENNE RETRIEVER CLUB   c/o
Mrs. Dorothy I. Hogan, Route 1, Box 535, Cheyenne, Wyo.

SHERIDAN RETRIEVER CLUB   c/o
Mr. V. J. Mediate, 205 Rice Ave., Sheridan, Wyo.

And last, but by no means least, the two clubs responsible for the two Championship trials held each year:

NATIONAL RETRIEVER FIELD TRIAL CLUB   c/o
Dr. George H. Gardner, 720 North Michigan Ave., Chicago 11, Ill.

NATIONAL AMATEUR RETRIEVER CLUB   c/o
Mr. K. K. Williams, 2370 N. 32d St., Milwaukee, Wis.

Glossary of Field Trial Terms

Field trials and field trial people have a language all their own. To clarify the conversations you will hear at any field trial, the following terms and their meanings are included.

BLIND	Bird put down before dog comes on line.
BLINKING THE BIRD	Dog sees bird, but fails to retrieve it.
BREAK	Dog attempts to retrieve without being sent by handler.
BUTTON JOB	Going directly to bird.
COLD BLIND	No shot and dog is sent for blind.
COLD HONOR	Dog honors before he retrieves his birds.
CREEPING	Dog inches forward as birds are being shot.
CROSSWIND	Wind blowing across direction dog is running.
DELAYED SHOT	Guns shoot bird, or birds, and dog retrieves; another bird is then shot while dog is still on line.
DELIVER	Bring to hand.
DIVERSION	Used with a blind; marked bird is shot and retrieved before dog is sent for the blind.
DOUBLE	Two shot birds.
DOWNWIND	Wind blowing in direction dog is running.
DRY SHOT	Guns shoot, but no bird is thrown; a dry shot is used in connection with some blinds.

FADE	Dog veers with wind or terrain rather than holding his original line.
GUNS	Those who shoot the birds.
GUNS FADE, OR RETIRE	Guns disappear after they shoot.
HANDLER	Person who is running dog.
HANDLING	Using whistle and hand signals to direct dog.
HARD-MOUTHED	Dog who chews or squashes bird.
HEEL, OR HEELING	Dog beside you while walking or on line.
HONOR	Dog retrieves his birds and then sits while the next dog is tested.
IN THE HOLE	Dog and handler awaiting their turn.
LAUNCH YOUR DOG	Get your dog well out before handling him.
LINE	The place from which a dog is sent to retrieve as designated by the Judges.
LINE-JOB	Direct route to blind with no whistles.
LINE MANNERS	Dog's behavior on line.
LINING A DOG	Putting your hand out in the direction of a bird and then sending him along that line.
MARKED BIRD	Bird shot while dog is on line watching.
MARSHAL	Chairman, responsible for mechanics of trial.
NUMBER	Dog receives a number when entered in a trial and it is then used rather than his name.
OFF LINE	Not under judgment.
ON LINE	Dog under judgment.
OVER AND UNDER	Birds fall in a line with dog, far one first.
PICK UP	Dog fails to complete and the Judges ask the handler to call him in.
PLAYING THE WIND	Dog using the wind to advantage in finding his bird.
POP	When dog stops and looks back to handler for directions without reason.
POPPER	Gun who shoots while dead or shackled bird is thrown.

RECAST	Dog is sent, fails to go or only goes a few feet and must be sent again.
RE-RUN	A bad fall or other unequality causes the dog to be retested.
SCRATCH, SCRATCHED	A dog is entered, but later withdrawn.
SERIES	One of the several tests that collectively make a stake.
SINGLE	One shot bird.
SKYLARKING	Dog running around without purpose.
SPOOKY	A dog that is shy or afraid.
STAKE	One of the several separate classifications that comprise to make a trial.
STEADY	Dog stays put until sent.
STEWARD	Handy-andy, does what needs doing at trial.
STYLISH	A dog that exhibits speed, eagerness, etc.
SWITCH	When dog failing to locate the bird he went for, leaves that area and goes to the area of another bird.
TEST	*See* SERIES.
TRIPLE	Three shot birds.
UNDER AND OVER	Birds fall in a line with dog, short one first.
UP	The dog and handler on line.

Suppliers and Manufacturers of Quality Equipment

ABERCROMBIE & FITCH COMPANY   General equipment
9 North Wabash Avenue, Chicago, Illinois
362 Madison Avenue, New York, New York
220 Post Street, San Francisco, California

AIRBOURNE (MCKEE INDUSTRIES)   Crates
Box 90111, Airport Station, Los Angeles, California

KENNEL-AIRE   Crates and miscellaneous equipment
861 Clayland Street, St. Paul, Minnesota

SPORTING DOG EQUIPMENT COMPANY   General equipment
1817 N.W. 18th Avenue, Portland, Oregon

SPORTING DOG SPECIALTY COMPANY   General equipment
Spencerport, New York

E. W. UNDERHILL   Crates and dog houses
Lakeview, Katonah, New York

The publication for those interested in retrievers is:
FIELD TRIAL NEWS   c/o
Mr. John Fraser, Jr., 757 North Broadway, Milwaukee, Wisconsin